D0734335

The Lomond Guide to
# Scottish Castles

Dane Love

LOMOND BOOKS

*For my wife, Hazel, who visited virtually every castle with me.*

First published in 1998 for Lomond Books, 36 West Shore Road
Granton, EDINBURGH, EH5 1QD

Produced by Neil Wilson Publishing Ltd
303a The Pentagon Centre
36 Washington Street
GLASGOW
G3 8AZ

Tel: 0141-221-1117
Fax: 0141-221-5363

E-mail: *nwp@cqm.co.uk*
http://www.nwp.co.uk/

The author would like to thank the numerous owners and guides
for their assistance in answering questions put to them. All photographs are by the author, apart from those of Kisimul, Muness,
Noltland, Rowallan and Scalloway castles, which are courtesy of
Historic Scotland.

ISBN 094-778 2729

Printed in the United Arab Emirates

# Contents

Introduction ............................................................vii

**Aberdeen and the North-East**
Ballindalloch Castle ...........................................11
Balvenie Castle ...............................................12
Braemar Castle ...............................................13
Brodie Castle .................................................14
Castle Fraser .................................................15
Corgarff Castle ...............................................16
Craigievar Castle .............................................17
Crathes Castle ...............................................19
Darnaway Castle ..............................................20
Delgatie Castle ...............................................21
Drum Castle ..................................................22
Duffus Castle .................................................23
Dunnottar Castle .............................................24
Fyvie Castle ..................................................25
Glenbuchat Castle ............................................26
Huntly Castle ................................................27
Kildrummy Castle ............................................28
Leith Hall ....................................................30
Spynie Castle .................................................31
Tolquhon Castle ..............................................32

**Argyll and Bute**
Barcaldine Castle .............................................35
Carnasserie Castle ............................................36
Castle Sween .................................................37
Duart Castle ..................................................38
Dunstaffnage Castle ..........................................39
Inveraray Castle ..............................................40
Kilchurn Castle ...............................................41
Rothesay Castle ...............................................42
Skipness Castle ...............................................43
Torosay Castle ................................................44

## The Borders

Aikwood Tower ............................................. 47
Ayton Castle ............................................... 48
Drumlanrig's Tower ....................................... 49
Floors Castle ............................................. 50
Greenknowe Tower ......................................... 51
Hermitage Castle .......................................... 52
Neidpath Castle ........................................... 53
Smailholm Tower ........................................... 55
Thirlestane Castle ........................................ 56

## Dumfries and Galloway

Caerlaverock Castle ....................................... 59
Cardoness Castle .......................................... 60
Carsluith Castle .......................................... 61
Castle of St John ......................................... 62
Drumcoltran Tower ......................................... 63
Drumlanrig Castle ......................................... 64
Lochmaben Castle .......................................... 65
MacLellan's Castle ........................................ 66
Morton Castle ............................................. 67
Orchardton Tower .......................................... 68
Threave Castle ............................................ 69

## Dundee and Angus

Broughty Castle ........................................... 72
Edzell Castle ............................................. 73
Glamis Castle ............................................. 74

## Edinburgh, Lothians and Fife

Aberdour Castle ........................................... 77
Balgonie Castle ........................................... 78
Blackness Castle .......................................... 79
Craigmillar Castle ........................................ 80
Crichton Castle ........................................... 81
Dirleton Castle ........................................... 82
Edinburgh Castle .......................................... 83
Hailes Castle ............................................. 85
Kellie Castle ............................................. 86
Lauriston Castle .......................................... 87
Lennoxlove Castle ......................................... 88
Ravenscraig Castle ........................................ 89
St Andrews Castle ......................................... 90
Scotstarvit Tower ......................................... 91
Tantallon Castle .......................................... 92

## Glasgow, Lanarkshire and the West of Scotland

Bothwell Castle ........................................... 95
Brodick Castle ............................................ 96

Craignethan Castle ...............................................97
Crookston Castle ...............................................98
Culzean Castle ...............................................99
Dean Castle ...............................................100
Dumbarton Castle ...............................................101
Dundonald Castle ...............................................102
Kelburn Castle ...............................................103
Loch Doon Castle ...............................................104
Lochranza Castle ...............................................105
Newark Castle ...............................................106

## Inverness, the Highlands and Islands
Armadale Castle ...............................................109
Castle of Old Wick ...............................................110
Castle Stuart ...............................................111
Cawdor Castle ...............................................112
Dunrobin Castle ...............................................113
Dunvegan Castle ...............................................114
Eilean Donan Castle ...............................................115
Strome Castle ...............................................117
Urquhart Castle ...............................................118

## Orkney and Shetland
Muness Castle ...............................................120
Noltland Castle ...............................................121
Scalloway Castle ...............................................122

## Perth and Kinross
Balhousie Castle ...............................................125
Balvaird Castle ...............................................126
Blair Castle ...............................................127
Burleigh Castle ...............................................128
Castle Menzies ...............................................129
Elcho Castle ...............................................130
Huntingtower Castle ...............................................131
Lochleven Castle ...............................................132

## Stirling and Central
Alloa Tower ...............................................135
Castle Campbell ...............................................136
Doune Castle ...............................................137
Menstrie Castle ...............................................138
Stirling Castle ...............................................139

## The Western Isles
Kisimul Castle ...............................................142

## Castles Open Irregularly Or By Appointment
Balfluig Castle ...............................................144
Castle Stalcaire ...............................................144
Claypotts Castle ...............................................145

Comlongon Castle …………………………………145
Coxton Tower …………………………………………146
Craigston Castle ………………………………………147
Ferniehirst Castle ……………………………………147
Gilnockie Tower ………………………………………148
Kilravock Castle ………………………………………148
Minard Castle …………………………………………149
Monzie Castle …………………………………………149
Sorn Castle ……………………………………………150
Towie Barclay Castle ………………………………151

**Castles In Care**
Auchindoun Castle ……………………………………153
Cadzow Castle ………………………………………153
Castle Girnigoe and Sinclair ……………………153
Castle of Park …………………………………………154
Clackmannan Tower …………………………………155
Inverlochy Castle ……………………………………155
Preston Tower …………………………………………156
Rowallan Castle ………………………………………156

**Glossary** ……………………………………………157
**Index to Main Entries** ………………………159

# Introduction

SCOTLAND is famous for its castles. There are thousands of them, varying in condition from fragmentary ruins to massive baronial mansions which are still inhabited. This book details the hundred or so castles which are officially open to the public. The reader will note that many other ruins are accessible, but these are often private or in a dangerous condition, and due care should be taken if a visit is proposed.

The oldest stone castles in Scotland date from the 13th century. These were simple curtain walls, often containing wooden buildings within. One of the most typical of this type is Castle Sween, in Knapdale. In the more prosperous parts of Scotland, where the lowland farms produced a better income, dressed ashlar buildings such as Dirleton and Caerlaverock were built, and these are fine examples of their period. In the 14th century tall keeps, or tower-houses, became the more normal type of castle, and examples of this type of building can be seen at Threave, or Alloa.

In 1535 King James V decreed that all who owned land valued at £100 Scots should build a 'tour of defence', and it is from this time that many of Scotland's unique tower houses date. Hundreds of these towers survive, often still inhabited, though others are in ruins, and many more are incorporated into later buildings. Being comparatively small, these towers still make suitable homes, and in recent years dozens of them have been restored.

Later on, builders changed the plan by building the stair in a wing (previously it was located in the thickness of the wall) and thus produced the common L-plan tower. An unaltered example is Scotstarvit Tower, where the stair jamb projects from one corner, and climbs right up to the battlements. Some L-plan castles were slightly altered by having the jamb slightly off-set, allowing shot-holes to protect a second external wall. The Z-plan castle has towers at opposite corners, allowing the main walls of the castle to be protected. A very fine example of this style can be seen at Claypotts in Dundee.

The tradition for castle-living in Scotland has never really left us.

In the 18th century architects like Robert Adam were building country mansions like Culzean in the castle-style, and in the early-19th
century Sir Walter Scott reawakened an interest in Scottish history,
resulting in yet more castle-building. The neo-baronial architectural
style became extremely popular, and modern castles like Ayton and
Torosay continued the tradition. Though large castles of this type are
no longer constructed, smaller baronial towers are still being constructed and copy the styles of the 16th and 17th centuries.

Many of the ancient and royal castles of Scotland are now protected by Historic Scotland, which is a government agency responsi-
ble for their preservation and upkeep. The National Trust for
Scotland is an independent trust which cares for many more castles,
and it is often worth becoming members of both organisations. If
you would like to join, please contact: Membership Services, The
National Trust for Scotland, 5 Charlotte Square, EDINBURGH,
EH2 4DU. Tel: 0131 226 5922. Historic Scotland can be contacted
at Longmore House, Salisbury Place, EDINBURGH, EH9 1SH.
Tel: 0131 668 8800. A number of councils also have castles in their
care, as do various clan associations. The rest tend to be privately
owned, whether by an individual or a charitable trust.

## HOW TO USE THIS BOOK

Entries in this book are listed region by region alphabetically by
castle name. For the quickest access to each castle, please refer to the
index on page 148. In front of each name is a symbol which gives a
rough guide to the castle's condition:

🏠 Indicates that the castle is roofed and lived in, or furnished
as such.

🏛 Indicates that the castle is roofed but empty, or has museum
exhibits within it.

🏚 Indicates that the castle is in a ruinous condition.

## LOCATION

The postal address of the castle is given, followed by the relevant
Ordnance Survey Landranger map number and National Grid Reference.

## FACILITIES

A series of symbols indicate the following:

📖 Guidebook available.
♠ Castle has attractive Gardens.
⊞ Giftshop.
♿ Reasonable access for disabled.
☕ Cafe or snacks on sale.
✕ Restaurant or meals available.
🚻 Toilets.

## OWNER

The owner of the castle (or the curator in the case of many Historic Scotland properties) is named, along with a telephone number for further inquiries.

## OPEN OR CLOSED?

A rough guide to the opening days is given. For more detailed information on opening hours and current prices, the reader should contact the castle by telephoning the number given beforehand to avoid disappointment

## ENTRY

The following symbols give an approximate indication of price bands for adult admission:

◑   Admission up to £2.50.
◓   Admission between £2.50 and £5.00.
◐   Admission £5.00 and over.

## CASTLE HISTORY

Information on the history, architecture and owners of the castle, as well as details on what the visitor may see or which rooms are open to the public, follows.

## GLOSSARY

On pages 157/158 some of the more common terms are defined in order to aid understanding of the castle histories.

Dane Love
Auchinleck
January 1998

# Aberdeen and
# the North-East

# ☗ *Ballindalloch Castle*

| | |
|---|---|
| *Location* | Bridge of Avon, Aberlour, Banffshire, AB37 9AX. |
| | OS Map 28: NJ 178365. |
| *Facilities* | ⬚▲🚻🚻🛆✕🚻 |
| *Owner* | Oliver Russell. |
| *Tel* | 01807 500206. |
| *Open* | Apr-Sep, Mon-Sun. |
| *Entry* | ◑ |

Ballindalloch is a particularly fine building, lovingly cared for by the Russell and Macpherson-Grant families. Historically a Grant seat, it became Macpherson-Grant, until the daughter married Oliver Russell. Their son, Guy, has assumed the surname Macpherson-Grant to continue the family name.

The corner tower, which formed a Z-plan castle, was probably built in 1546, which date appears on a fireplace. Since then the castle has been extended a number of times – in 1770, 1850 and 1878. The last extension was removed in 1965.

A delightful confection of turrets and dormer windows, Ballindalloch opens a wide selection of rooms to the public. From the entrance hall, with its umbrella ceiling, one enters the drawing room and then the Laird's Smoking Room. The library has a very fine collection of over 2,500 volumes. The dining room is located in what was the great hall of the original tower and the panelling of pine and the ceiling plasterwork are copied from casts of the ceiling at Craigievar.

The tour continues through the nursery, the Pink Tower (reputedly haunted), the Old Tower with its spiral staircase which changes direction half-way up and the dungeon passage. The latter corridor is also haunted by the ghost of General James Grant who drinks from the wine cellar located in the old dungeon, which still has its heavy door and massive padlock. The castle displays a spectacular collection of paintings, furniture and antiques throughout.

The grounds are extensive, with the lawns spreading down to the confluence of the Avon and Spey. The doocot is dated 1696 and has 844 nest boxes. Craftsmen work in various buildings on the estate, and there is an audio-visual room.

## Balvenie Castle

| | |
|---|---|
| *Location* | Dufftown, Banffshire. |
| | OS Map 28: NJ 326409. |
| *Facilities* | 🏠 ♿ ♿ |
| *Owner* | Hammond Burke Nicholson/Historic Scotland. |
| *Tel* | 01340 820121 |
| *Open* | Apr-Sep, Mon-Sun. |
| *Entry* | ☺ |

Balvenie is entered through an unusual double-leafed yett. The pend passes through the 4th Earl of Atholl's Lodging, which has a fine round tower at the external corner and a smaller stair turret in the inner re-entrant. The cobbled courtyard is surrounded by buildings, some more ruinous than others.

The original castle, known as Mortlach, was built by the Comyns in the 12th century. Part of this may survive in the present courtyard, but alterations were made to it over the centuries. In the 16th century Balvenie was extended by the addition of a domestic block (to left of entrance). The Atholl lodging was added to the right of this between 1547-57, the windows having decorative stonework and small oriels at second floor level. There are heraldic panels on the walls. The ruinous west range probably dates from the 15th century and then contained a kitchen, brewhouse, and great chamber with the hall above. Only low walls of these buildings survive. In the courtyard is a deep well.

Balvenie was originally a Comyn seat, followed by the Douglases, but in 1470 it was granted to John Stewart, later 1st Earl of Atholl. Mary, Queen of Scots stayed in 1562. The castle remained in Stewart hands until 1610 after which it had numerous owners until bought by Alexander Duff. The castle was used as a garrison during the Jacobite rebellion but was abandoned following Culloden, as Duff had erected a classical Balvenie House nearby in 1724. The castle was placed in state care in 1929 by the Duke of Fife.

##  Braemar Castle

| | |
|---|---|
| *Location* | Braemar, Aberdeenshire, AB5 4EX. |
| | OS Map 43: NJ 156924. |
| *Facilities* | 🏠 ♿ ☕ |
| *Owner* | Captain Farquharson of Invercauld. |
| *Tel* | 013398 741219/741224. |
| *Open* | Easter-Oct, Sat-Thur. |
| *Entry* | ◐ |

The original tower was erected in 1628 by John Erskine, Earl of Mar, as a bulwark against the power of the neighbouring Farquharsons. In 1689 it was burned by John Farquharson of Inverey. Acquired in

1732 by John Farquharson, the castle was leased in 1748 for 99 years to the Government who restored and altered the tower (notably the star-shaped wall and tops of the turrets). They used it as a garrison for soldiers following the Jacobite rising. The alterations were supervised by John Adam, elder son of William and brother of Robert, all notable Scots architects. It was later converted to a private residence, and visited by Queen Victoria.

From the entrance door one climbs to the dining room which has a few Jacobite relics. Adjoining are the Pink Bedroom, dressing room and bathroom. The drawing room has graffiti left by soldiers – Sergt. John Chestnut, 1797, and others. The four poster room is a bed chamber with two closets in the turrets. The morning room contains the world's largest Cairngorm stone, weighing 52 pounds, and Canadian Indian objects. The vaulted kitchen has various relics including an early fridge. Rooms on the ground floor contain exhibits of military relics, taxidermy, children's toys, foreign costumes, flags and standards and Farquharson memorabilia. There is a charter of 1633 by the Earl of Mar in favour of Farquharson of Invercauld, a yett and a prison pit with bones. Outside the star wall is a stone cheese-press.

# Brodie Castle

| | |
|---|---|
| *Location* | Brodie, Forres, Moray, IV36 0TE. OS Map 27: NH 979577. |
| *Facilities* | |
| *Owner* | National Trust for Scotland. |
| *Tel* | 01309 641371. |
| *Open* | Apr-Sep, Mon-Sun; Oct, Sat-Sun. |
| *Entry* | |

The Brodies have been at Brodie since 1160 when Malcolm IV endowed the lands. The 25th Chief, Ninian Brodie of that Ilk, had the castle passed to the Trust in 1980 but continues to live there and takes an active part in the running of the estate.

From the entrance hall, with the guardroom off, one enters the library, where the pillars are merely decorative and hold books. The secondary stair, with its stain-glass window of the Brodie arms, leads to the dining room, the ceiling of which is a rich fenestration of wooden carvings. The Blue Sitting Room has a vaulted plaster roof. The Red Drawing Room was the castle's original high hall, and is now adorned with a gothic fireplace. The drawing room follows, then a series of bedrooms, then a nursery and on to the main staircase. The kitchen is fitted out to reproduce its look when it was added to the castle in early Victorian times.

Brodie as it stands today owes much to the architect William Burn who enlarged it in 1824. However, the original Z-plan castle of 1567 survives, and the harling blends the various additions beautifully. In 1645 the castle had been partially destroyed by fire by Lord Lewis Gordon during the Montrose campaigns. Alexander, 19th Brodie, was the Lord Lyon King of Arms, and his family's interest in arms is clear from those on display.

The policies of 175 acres are also owned by the Trust, and the grounds are richly wooded. In the spring there is also a magnificent display of daffodils, established by the 24th Laird, who bred over 400 varieties himself. The ninth-century Rodney Stone, a Pictish symbol stone, stands by the drive.

#  *Castle Fraser*

| | |
|---|---|
| *Location* | Sauchen, Inverurie, Aberdeenshire, AB51 7LD. OS Map 38: NJ 723125. |
| *Facilities* | □ ▲ ⊞ ⚲ ♿ |
| *Owner* | National Trust for Scotland. |
| *Tel* | 01330 833463. |
| *Open* | Easter; May-Sep, Mon-Sun; Oct, Sat-Sun. |
| *Entry* | ● |

Castle Fraser was erected between 1575-1635 by Michael Fraser with assistance from the Master Mason, Thomas Leiper. It was known as Muchall-in-Mar until 1695. The castle was completed by his heir, Andrew Fraser, 1st Lord Fraser. The main block is a Z-plan tower of five storeys, to the north of which is a courtyard with double-storeyed 'Laigh Biggin's' and gateway. The tower has a square and round projection. The latter is of the castle's most notable features and the roof is reached through an attractive cap-house. It affords excellent views not only of the surrounding countryside but also of the turrets and roofs of the adjoining buildings.

Tours of the castle take one through the vaulted kitchen and laigh hall. On the first floor is the great hall with its large fireplace, laird's lug, and the original doorway, which is now blocked. On the same floor is the dining room and the Peacock Parlour or smoking room. The latter room is located in the round tower, but is square in shape. On the third floor are the Green, North, Worked and Tower rooms, which are mostly bedrooms. The fourth floor has the Pink Room, Red and Blue turrets and the library (the largest room in the castle). This has decoration of 1839 when it was altered by the architect John Smith. Descending by a second stair one reaches the Bailiff's Room on the second floor. This has a squint which looks down into the great hall. A small room adjoining is said to have been a chapel.

Castle Fraser remained in Fraser ownership until 1921 when it was bought by the 1st Viscount Cowdray for his son, Hon. Clive Pearson. It passed to his daughter, Lavinia, who married Major Michael Smiley. They gifted the castle to the Trust in 1976.

## 🏠 *Corgarff Castle*

| | |
|---|---|
| *Location* | Cock Bridge, Strathdon, Aberdeenshire. |
| | OS Map 37: NO 254087. |
| *Facilities* | 🚻 |
| *Owner* | Historic Scotland. |
| *Tel* | 01975 651460. |
| *Open* | Apr-Sep, Mon-Sun; Oct-Mar, Sat-Sun. |
| *Entry* | ☛ |

Originally part of the Earldom of Mar, James IV annexed the estates in 1435 and granted the 'Foresta de Corgarf' to Alexander Elphinstone.

In 1571 the castle was set alight, killing Margaret Forbes and 24 others. The Erskines of Mar regained control in 1626. Montrose occupied the building in 1645. The Jacobites burned it in 1689; the Hanoverians in 1716. It was then granted to the Forbes but in 1748 it was taken over by the Government and converted into a military barracks. The tower was repaired, pavilions added, and the star-shaped curtain-wall erected. Inside its cobbled courtyard is the round cistern. In 1750 40 privateers, three corporals, two sergeants and a lieutenant occupied the building. It was abandoned by the troops in 1831.

The external stair leads to the first floor where the curator often has a peat fire burning. A wooden stair replaces the stone turnpike, leading to the second floor, which has been restored as a military dormitory, with beds, eating area, and restored ceiling graffiti! The upper floors are bare, apart from wall displays, and are sometimes used for exhibitions. The garret is adorned with a flagstaff.

The ground floor of the tower is vaulted. The west pavilion houses a whisky still, as the castle acted as a distillery and shooting lodge for a time. By the 1900s the building was ruinous. In 1961 it was passed into care by Sir Edmund and Lady Stockdale of Delnadamph.

# Craigievar Castle

| | |
|---|---|
| *Location* | Muir of Fowlis, Alford, Aberdeenshire, AB33 8JF. OS Map 37: NJ 567095. |
| *Facilities* | |
| *Owner* | National Trust for Scotland. |
| *Tel* | 013398 83635. |
| *Open* | May-Sep, Mon-Sun. |
| *Entry* | |

Perhaps one of the finest and least altered castles in Scotland,

Craigievar was completed in 1626 by William Forbes, better known as 'Danzig Willie' from his Baltic trade connections. It remained in the same family, later to become Forbes-Sempill and Lords Sempill, until it was sold to a group of buyers who gifted it to the Trust in 1963. L-shaped in plan, the castle has its entrance in the re-entrant tower. The building rises six storeys in height, and the last two are decorated externally by a profusion of turrets and corbels. The tower rises to a seventh floor.

From the entrance doorway one can visit the 'dungeon', kitchen and pantry, the latter being located beneath the wide stairway leading to the great hall, which passes through two floors. The great hall is vaulted and has a decorative plaster ceiling and overmantel dated 1626, the latter with the Royal arms. At one end is a split minstrels' gallery, located over the screens passage. On the same floor is the pine-panelled withdrawing room and the 'Prophet's Chamber'. A small spiral stair then leads up to the Tartan Bedroom and ante-room. The third floor has two main bedrooms with ante-rooms off, one of which has an altered box-bed converted into a small bathroom. Further bedrooms are located on the fourth floor, one of which was a nursery for a time. There are attractive bays in the turrets of the Blue Room. The fifth floor has a gallery, containing old charters and genealogical information, and a servants' bedroom. A lesser spiral stair descends down to the great hall.

Only one wall and turret of a former barmkin wall which surrounded the castle, survive.

# ⓘ *Crathes Castle*

| | |
|---|---|
| *Location* | Crathes, Banchory, Kincardineshire, AB31 3QJ. |
| | OS Maps 38, 45: NO 734968. |
| *Facilities* | ⊞▲⊞♿✕♿ |
| *Owner* | National Trust for Scotland. |
| *Tel* | 01330 844525. |
| *Open* | Apr-Oct, Mon-Sun. |
| *Entry* | ● |

The lands of Leys were granted to the Burnett family in 1323 by Robert the Bruce, along with a horn, still preserved in the great hall. The family built the present tower in 1553-96 to which was added a later wing. This, and Victorian additions, were destroyed by fire in 1966, and only the Queen Anne wing was partially rebuilt. The castle was gifted to the Trust in 1951 by Sir James Burnett of Leys, Bart.

Tours commence in the Queen Anne wing but quickly reach the original tower. Here are the vaulted kitchens and a dining room. A turnpike from the original entrance, with yett, leads to the Great Hall, which has painted alcoves. The large window was added in the 1870s. The stair chamber is the first room to be reached which has the original painted ceilings for which Crathes is noted. The Victorian bedroom is furnished with items from that period, with a notable triple picture of three views, depending from where it is seen. The laird's bedroom contains a massive four-poster carved from oak. The Nine Nobles Room is so-called from the painted ceiling depicting, among others, Alexander the Great, King Arthur and Joshua.

The haunted Green Lady's Room also has a painted ceiling and wall tapestries. Here the skeleton of a child was found beneath the fire hearth. The Family Room contains items associated with the Burnetts. On the top floor of the castle runs the gallery, the ceiling of which is panelled in oak. This was for a time the library. The Muses Room also has a painted ceiling and old stitched samplers. The Stone Hall contains a small selection of weapons. Exit is made by way of a wide staircase in the Queen Anne wing back to the main door.

## Darnaway Castle

| | |
|---|---|
| *Location* | Darnaway, Forres, Moray. |
| | OS Map 27: NH 994550. |
| *Facilities* | None. |
| *Owner* | Earl of Moray. |
| *Tel* | 01309 641469. |
| *Open* | Jul-Aug, |
| *Entry* | ◗ |

Visitors should book tours at Darnaway Country Centre at Tearie, just off the A96, from where the estate minibus drives visitors to the castle. The Darnaway seen on arrival is a Gothic mansion of 1802-12, designed by Alexander Laing of Edinburgh for the 9th and 10th Earls of Moray. It cost £12,000 to build. The old castle was to have been restored, but when work commenced in 1788 various parts of it collapsed with near-fatal results. It was decided to build anew. However, the great hall of the old castle was recognised for its unique character, and the architect was instructed to incorporate it in the new building.

From the front door one reaches the entrance hall, which has a fine collection of family portraits. To the left is the drawing room, followed by the dining room. To the rear of the castle is the great, or Randolph's, hall with its magnificent 15th-century oak collar-beam truss roof. It measures 90ft by 35ft. Standards of various Moray ancestors hang there. On the wall, usually hidden behind doors, is the famous painting of the Bonnie Earl of Moray, of ballad fame, showing him with the lacerations and scars received when he was murdered in 1591 by the Earl of Huntly at Donibristle.

Darnaway had been owned by the Dunbar, Douglas and Gordon families, until the Stuarts acquired it in 1562, and have kept it ever since.

## Delgatie Castle

| Location | Delgatie, Turriff, Aberdeenshire, AB53 8ED. |
|---|---|
| | OS Map 29: NJ 754506. |
| *Facilities* | ▲ ♨ ♿ |
| *Owner* | Delgatie Castle Trust |
| *Tel* | 01888 562750/563479. |
| *Open* | Apr-Oct, Mon-Sun. |
| *Entry* | ◖ |

Reputedly dating back to around 1030, what stands of Delgatie today dates from 1570-9. Wings were added in 1743, the most westerly containing a Chapel. The grounds have a garden, the Thomson Memorial Fountain of 1918 and various carved stones.

Delgatie was taken from the Earl of Buchan in 1314 and granted to the Hays, later Earls of Erroll. Sold to Garden of Troup in 1763, the Duff Earls of Fife later acquired the estate, but it has since returned to Hay ownership. Mary, Queen of Scots stayed for three days in 1562.

The castle was threatened with demolition but Captain John Hay (1906-97) decided instead to live there and commence its restoration.

The tour of the house is virtually an ascent of the tall spiral staircase (97 treads), visiting each room which extends off it. From the vaulted ground floor one visits the ballroom with oriel window, the withdrawing room, the anteroom and Tulip Room, the latter having an old aumbry and painted ceiling beams of 1593. There are various bedrooms to be seen, especially the Romaise Room which has a painted ceiling of 1597. The bedroom above, called the Attock Fort, has a painted ceiling of 1955!

Delgatie shows its antiquity, and its owner's interest in stonemasonry and heraldry. Various carved stones were the work of John Hay, including Elephant corbels and coats of arms. There are a number of fine portraits, antiques and cannon.

# Drum Castle

| Location | Drumoak, Banchory, Kincardineshire, AB31 5EY.<br>OS Map 38: NJ 796005. |
|---|---|
| Facilities | ▢▲⊞♨✕☕ |
| Owner | National Trust for Scotland. |
| Tel | 01330 811204. |
| Open | Easter; May-Sep, Mon-Sun; Oct, Sat-Sun. |
| Entry | ● |

The old tower of Drum is believed to be one of the three oldest towers surviving in Scotland. Adjoining it is a large wing of 1619 and some Victorian additions. The old tower was the work of Richard Cementarius, Master Mason to the King in the late-13th century. The ground floor vault has a well. The lands were granted to William Irvine in 1323 by Robert the Bruce and remained in their ownership (latterly Forbes-Irvine) until they were given to the Trust in 1976.

Tours commence in the Victorian entrance hall and lead to the drawing room, restored in Victorian times with an oak ceiling. Off it is the Irvine Room, with genealogical books associated with the clan. The dining room is followed by the Business Room with the Muniment Room off it – it is locked behind a steel door. Tours continue through the Green Bedroom and closet, the Chintz Room and Cross Chamber to the vaulted library, located in the laigh hall of the old tower. The oldest book is a history of Italy dating from the 16th century. The gallery is a corridor leading back to the main stairs; it contains relics associated with Prince Charlie and Mary, Queen of Scots. On the ground floor are vaulted kitchens, sculleries and a tearoom. Closed to the public are the north wing, which contains the former brew house and gateway. Near the castle is the heavily-restored 16th-century chapel.

## Duffus Castle

| Location | Old Duffus, Duffus, Elgin, Moray. |
| --- | --- |
| | OS Map 28: NJ 189673. |
| Facilities | &#9855; |
| Owner | Historic Scotland. |
| Tel | 0131 668 8800. |
| Open | All Year, Mon-Sun. |
| Entry | Free. |

Duffus stands on a man-made motte hill in the middle of a circular moat in the midst of an agricultural plain. This was at one time the huge Loch Spynie which has gradually been drained over the centuries. Duffus dates in part to 1151. It was at first a Royal stronghold, but it was granted to Hugo Freskin from Strabock in West Lothian who adopted the de Moravia or Moray name. The castle was held for a time by the English, but was burned by Scots in 1297. The keep of the castle may date from the rebuilding. In 1452 the castle was destroyed again, after which the hall and various other buildings were added. The castle was abandoned in the late-17th century when the first Duffus House was erected a mile away.

On entering the grounds of the castle from the car-park it is worth striking left to follow the moat round to the ancient bridge and original entry to the castle. The remains of an old cobbled roadway rise gently to the bailey wall. Lesser courtyard buildings lie in ruins below the main keep. Steps lead up the motte to the narrow entrance which passes through the thick walls. Through it one sees at close proximity the massive corner of the keep which has slid down the side of the hill, the foundations being weak. It is a weird sight, with the latrine within the wall thickness remaining intact. Elsewhere on the tower walls one can see other signs of subsidence, especially at one window, where the lintels have moved about nine inches. The hall was rebuilt in the 15th century. The castle of Duffus was bought by Sir Archibald Dunbar in 1705, but it was by then abandoned.

## Dunnottar Castle

| | |
|---|---|
| *Location* | Stonehaven, Kincardineshire, AB3 2TL. |
| | OS Map 45: NO 881839. |
| *Facilities* | |
| *Owner* | Hon. Charles A. Pearson, Dunecht Estates. |
| *Tel* | 01569 762173. |
| *Open* | Apr-Oct, Mon-Sun; Nov-Mar, Mon-Fri. |
| *Entry* | |

This is a vast and impressive ruin perched on a great rocky headland. A steep path leads down the cliffside and up to the entrance gate, protected by large gunloops from the guardroom. The way continues through two tunnels to the grassed courtyard, with bowling green to the north and kirkyard to the south (with one tiny grave from 1685).

The buildings round the quadrangle and large well comprise the Silver House (re-roofed in 1927), with seven chambers below what was the 15th-century ballroom. The north and east range have a series of vaults which contain a wine cellar, kitchen, brewery, stores and the Whigs Vault. 122 men and 45 women were imprisoned in the Whigs Vault in 1685, and some died in making an escape. The remains of the 13th-century chapel are the oldest part of the castle. Over the vaults are the Countess and Marischal suites, the latter with armorial lintel over the fireplace and old stone clock-face. The restored dining room has a memorial over the fire commemorating the fact that the Honours of Scotland (Crown jewels) were kept here from 1651 until 1652. Waterton's Lodging dates from 1574; the stables and smithy are south of it. The keep is of the 14th century, with the lower floor vaulted and the great hall over. Beyond is the Wallace Door of 1297, a small museum room over Benholm's Lodging, the Lion's Den and the descent to entrance pend.

Dunnottar was the seat of the Keiths, Earls Marischal, until 1716 when the 10th Earl had his estates forfeited for his Jacobite adherences. Sold to the York Buildings Company, the castle was stripped and de-roofed. In 1919 J.W. Guy Innes sold the ruins to Viscountess Cowdray who undertook partial restoration. They remain the property of her descendants.

## ⓘ *Fyvie Castle*

| | |
|---|---|
| *Location* | Fyvie, Turriff, Aberdeenshire, AB53 8JS. |
| | OS Map 29: NJ 764393. |
| *Facilities* | ▲□ ♨ ☕ ♿ ⊞ |
| *Owner* | National Trust for Scotland. |
| *Tel* | 01651 891266. |
| *Open* | Apr-Sep, Mon-Sun; Oct, Sat-Sun. |
| *Entry* | ◗ |

Now a great Z-plan castle, the oldest part of Fyvie dates from the 13th century. Each successive laird has added to the building, to give the Preston, Meldrum, Seton, Gordon and Leith towers, in order of erection. Each alteration seems to have added a new kitchen, the older one being converted into something else – the billiard room for example.

The gallery and drawing room in the Leith and Gordon towers, dating from 1900, are two of the finest Edwardian rooms in Britain, having a barrel-vaulted ceiling and pipe organ. The great wheel stair, ten feet wide, is also notable, and built by the 1st Earl of Dunfermline. The whole building is covered with the arms of Lord Leith's ancestors.

The castle has a curse, causing the death of the laird and blindness of his wife should he try and enter the secret chamber below the Charter Room. In this room is a case containing a 'Weeping Stone', which over the centuries has oozed water at intervals.

Alexander Leith made his fortune in the Illinois Steel Company. He bought the castle in 1885 for £175,000. There are many American associations with the building. Sir Andrew Forbes-Leith sold Fyvie to the Trust in 1984.

## Glenbuchat Castle

| | |
|---|---|
| *Location* | Glenbuchat, Strathdon, Aberdeenshire. |
| | OS Map 37: NJ 397149. |
| *Facilities* | None. |
| *Owner* | Historic Scotland. |
| *Tel* | 0131 668 8800. |
| *Open* | All Year, Mon-Sun. |
| *Entry* | Free. |

This is an attractive Z-plan tower house, built in 1590 by John Gordon and Helen Carnegie whose names appeared on a worn lintel over the door with the motto NOCHT ON EARTH REMAINS BOT FAME. Built of random-rubble, the tower has sandstone dressings and two notable squinch arches supporting stair towers. There are two round and two square corbelled turrets at the corners, and the gables are crow-stepped. Glenbuchat (or Glenbucket) was owned by the Gordons until 1738 when John Gordon, a noted Jacobite, had it forfeited. It was sold to Lord Braco, later Earl of Fife. The roof was removed shortly after 1840.

The ground floor is vaulted and comprises a kitchen with salt boxes, gunloops, slop chute and adjoining pantry. A wide turnpike stair from the door leads to the first floor. This may be a later alteration. The first floor has the former great hall, which in 1701 was divided into a dining room and drawing room. Stumps of the wooden joists survive in some places. An adjoining chamber has a closet and wall cupboard. Over the dining room was a room with a large pair of windows. Remains of lesser spiral stairs remain.

The Duke of Fife sold the ruins to Henry Burra. Castle Park was gifted to the nation on 18th September 1948 by the Deeside Field Club.

## Huntly Castle

| | |
|---|---|
| *Location* | Castle Street, Huntly, Aberdeenshire. OS Map 29: NJ 531408. |
| *Facilities* | |
| *Owner* | Historic Scotland. |
| *Tel* | 01466 793191. |
| *Open* | Apr-Sep, Mon-Sun; Oct-Mar, Sat-Thu. |
| *Entry* | |

The great heraldic doorway is the finest part of Huntly Castle. This rises to 33ft, and contains the arms of the 1st Marquis of Huntly and his wife; the arms of the monarch, James VI and a device showing the five wounds of Christ and the glory of Christ risen. Over this is a figure of St Michael. Executed in red sandstone, the 'frontispiece' has been described as the 'most splendid heraldic doorway in the British Isles'.

Huntly Castle itself is just as interesting, for here can be seen three stages in castle development (the fourth stage, Huntly Castle Lodge, is now a hotel) on the same site. The motte stands to one side. The foundations of the 15th-century L-planned castle lay within the courtyard, and the 16th-century range forms the greatest remnant.

The lower part of the palace range has vaulted cellars and a dungeon with 'prisoners'. Over this are vaulted kitchen rooms, with the great chamber and hall above. The round tower contains the inner chamber with latrine, peep-hole and a bed recess. The upper hall and great chamber have impressive heraldic fireplaces.

The south front of Huntly has a unique suite of oriel windows with an inscribed frieze on the upper storey, which is almost as fine mason work as the doorway. This is inscribed GEORGE GORDOVN FIRST MARQVIS OF HVNTLIE 16 HENRIETTE STEVART MARQVESSE OF HVNTLIE 02. The bailey contains ruins of the kitchen, stable, bakery and brew house.

Huntly was granted to Sir Adam Gordon of Huntly in Berwickshire in the 14th century, after which place the castle was renamed, previously being called Strathbogie. It remained in the hands of the Gordons thereafter, who were created Earls, then Marquises, of Huntly. It was passed into care by the Duke of Richmond and Gordon in 1923.

## Kildrummy Castle

| | |
|---|---|
| *Location* | Kildrummy, Lumsden, Aberdeenshire. OS Map 37: NJ 455164. |
| *Facilities* | |
| *Owner* | Historic Scotland. |
| *Tel* | 01975 571331. |
| *Open* | Apr-Sep, Mon-Sun. |
| *Entry* | |

Kildrummy is one of the finest castle ruins in the north of Scotland. The greater part of the surviving ruins date from the 13th century and were probably erected by an Earl of Mar.

A path from the car park leads to the entrance gateway, reached by a bridge over the barbican. The gatehouse may have been built by an English mason, being similar to that at Harlech in Wales. There are another four great towers to the castle, built onto the wall of enceinte, creating a vast shield-shaped fortress. The Warden's Tower is the most complete, the Snow Tower having collapsed in 1805. Between the two is the ruin of the great gall, which was about 65ft long. The former chapel was a striking building, evidenced by the lancet windows of one gable which still survives. The need for an easterly orientation resulting in a projection outwith the line of the castle wall. A postern gate allowed an exit to fetch water.

Kildrummy remained in Mar hands until 1435 when James I took over the castle. It was then kept as a royal castle and administered by a constable. In 1507 the estates were granted to Lord Elphinstone and remained in his family's hands until 1626 when they were acquired by the Erskine Earls of Mar.

The castle was finally abandoned in 1716 when the Earl of Mar escaped to France following his failed Jacobite rebellion. In 1898 the ruins were acquired by James Ogston who did some stabilisation work and removal of debris. He died in 1931 and is commemorated by a plaque on the chapel gable. His niece placed the castle in care in 1951.

# ⌂ *Leith Hall*

| | |
|---|---|
| *Location* | Kennethmont, Huntly, Aberdeenshire, AB54 4NQ. OS Map 37: NJ 541298. |
| *Facilities* | ⌂ ♨ ⊞ ♿ ☕ |
| *Owner* | National Trust for Scotland. |
| *Tel* | 01464 831216. |
| *Open* | Easter; May-Sep, Mon-Sun; Oct, Sat-Sun. |
| *Entry* | ◗ |

Leith Hall was the seat of the Leith family, afterwards Leith-Hay, from 1650, when the oldest part of the castle was built. It was given to the Trust in 1945 by the Hon. Mrs Leith-Hay along with 286 acres of policies including the interesting gardens with Moon Gate and Half Round Stable. Her son and heir had been killed in a motor-cycle accident at the age of 21.

The oldest part of the Hall is in fact a tower house which has a vaulted lower storey. This has been added to over the years to create a chateau formed round a courtyard. The entrance to the house is to the east, from where tours circulate round the courtyard at first floor level. Rooms visited include the dining room, drawing room and a selection of bedrooms. On show are various Jacobite relics, including a writing set gifted by Bonnie Prince Charlie to Andrew Hay, as well as Hay's pardon from George III. It is thought to be the only such pardon in existence. There is an exhibition on the second floor of militaria associated with the Leith family. General Alexander Leith raised the Royal Aberdeenshire Regiment and was active in the Napoleonic wars. It was he who succeeded his uncle and adopted the Leith-Hay name. On the ground floor are the entrance hall (added in the 20th century), gift shop and Victorian kitchen, which doubles as a tea room. The house has a rich selection of portraits, furniture and a varied selection of tapestries and needlework.

Externally Leith Hall is a delightful white-harled confection, sporting conical turrets, carved arms and various dormer windows. The courtyard is reached through a pend from the west. A cheese-press is located within.

## Spynie Castle

| | |
|---|---|
| *Location* | Spynie, Lossiemouth, Moray. OS Map 28: NJ 231658. |
| *Facilities* | |
| *Owner* | Historic Scotland. |
| *Tel* | 01343 546358. |
| *Open* | Apr-Sep, Mon-Sun; Oct-Mar, Sat-Sun. |
| *Entry* | |

Known also as Spynie Palace, this was the seat of the Bishops of Moray from 1208 until the Reformation, after which the castle became ruinous. Mary, Queen of Scots stayed in 1562. The castle stands on the edge of what was once the great Spynie sea loch, with a harbour and small village, but this became silted and abandoned.

The great, or David's, tower is the most striking feature, rising six storeys in height, with walls tapering to the corbels. On the ground floor are vaulted cellars, one of which was the circular vault in a 14th-century castle. The first floor doorway leads to the interior, the floors of which have gone. However, one is impressed with the old masonry with mason's marks, and the modern restoration work which includes leaded windows, a concrete vaulted corridor and spiral stair. Some old plaster still adorns the walls. The stair leads to the parapet, which affords wide panoramas over the loch and Laich of Moray.

The courtyard is surrounded by other ruinous buildings, the most complete of which is the north-west tower, containing a doocot. The water gate is a notable feature, located between the kitchen ovens and the great hall (dates to 1500). The great hall has faces carved on two corbels, and a deep well at the east end. The east gate dates from the 15th century, and its external appearance is most attractive. The south range is basically now a single wall, but here can be seen an ornate piscina in what was the chapel.

## Tolquhon Castle

| | |
|---|---|
| *Location* | Pitmedden, Aberdeenshire. |
| | OS Map 38: NJ873286. |
| *Facilities* | 🏛 ⚏ ♿ ⚐ |
| *Owner* | Historic Scotland. |
| *Tel* | 01651 851286. |
| *Open* | Apr-Sep, Mon-Fri; Oct-Mar, Sat-Sun. |
| *Entry* | 🅟 |

An extensive and attractive ruin, Tolquhon was erected by the Forbes family around 1420. The tower of that date is surrounded by a large grassed courtyard which itself is surrounded by a barmkin wall with a notable gateway and fragmentary doocot. Adjoining the tower is a large extension of 1584-9 for William Forbes by Thomas Leiper. Tolquhon was sold by the family in 1716 to Lt-Col Francis Farquhar and the roofs fell in during the second half of the 19th century. It was latterly owned by the Earl of Aberdeen.

Guardrooms on either side of the gatehouse contain ornate gun-loops and various carvings, and one records the extension of the castle. Through the pend one sees the virtually complete round tower of the main block of the new works. The west range has brew houses on the vaulted ground floor and remains of a 58ft-long gallery above. In the right corner of the inner courtyard the main entrance leads up wide stairs to the first floor, from where the great hall is reached, the floor having fancy slabs. Beneath this room and adjoining laird's chamber are the kitchen, servery and wine cellar. The east range is more ruinous, but the east tower contains the bakehouse, over which is a chamber from where a trap door opens to the prison. In the old tower only part of the ground floor vault survives.

# Argyll and Bute

# 🏰 *Barcaldine Castle*

| | |
|---|---|
| *Location* | Benderloch, Argyll, PA37 1SA. |
| | OS Map 49: NM 908406. |
| *Facilities* | 🏠 ♿ 🚻 ☕ |
| *Owner* | Roderick Campbell, Yr. of Barcaldine. |
| *Tel* | 01631 720598. |
| *Open* | Easter, May-Sep, Mon-Sun; Apr, Oct, Sun-Fri. |
| *Entry* | ● |

Barcaldine Castle is a particularly attractive L-planned tower house, completed in 1609 by Sir Duncan Campbell of Glenorchy. The castle was an integral part of the Massacre of Glencoe, for MacIan of Glencoe was detained here for 24 hours in a plot to prevent him from swearing the oath of allegiance to William III in the given time.

The doorway at the foot of the re-entrant spiral stair still has its yett, c.1600. The stair leads up to the wainscoted great hall, which has an armorial fireplace. A secret doorway leads to the small stair up to the bedroom floor. The spiral stair goes to the top floor, where the library has displays on the Campbell family and the castle, as well as on the artist F.C.B. Cadell who lived here for a time. The tour descends to the Argyll room which is reputedly haunted by the 'Blue Lady' – Harriet Campbell, who is said to be heard playing the piano. The attractive Laird's Parlour is located off the great hall. In the corner of the hall a tiny stair drops to the ground floor vaults, now the location of the castle kitchen, dining room and stores. In the passage is a grating over the bottle dungeon.

Barcaldine was abandoned by the Campbells in 1735 when they moved to Barcaldine House. The estates were sold between 1836-43, but Sir Duncan Campbell bought the tower and restored it from 1896-1912. His, and earlier, arms are located on external walls.

## 🏠 *Carnasserie Castle*

| Location | Carnasserie, Kilmartin, Argyll. |
|---|---|
|  | OS Map 55: NM 838009. |
| Facilities | None. |
| Owner | Historic Scotland. |
| Tel | 0131 668 8800. |
| Open | All Year, Mon-Sun. |
| Entry | Free. |

A track from the car park climbs gradually uphill to the rocky knoll on which this grey tower stands, commanding views of Kilmartin glen. The tower, which was built as one despite looking as though it was extended, has interesting string courses, corbels and a carved panel over the re-entrant doorway. The ground floor had the kitchen, with a large fire and unusual water inlet and oven. The well is in the base of the tower. Spiral stairs climb up through the building at each end, but the floors have gone. Nevertheless, the wall-head walk is accessible, where Victorian graffiti and mason's marks can be seen. The castle has seven bedrooms, and the withdrawing room has an ornate fireplace.

The castle was built in the 1560s by John Carswell, who was granted the Protestant Bishopric of the Isles in 1567 and was translator of Knox's Liturgy into Gaelic. The castle passed to the Campbells of Auchinbreck in 1572; an old gateway to the orchard is dated 1681 with Sir Dougal Campbell's initials. He joined the Earl of Argyll in the Monmouth Rising of 1685 with the consequence that Carnasserie was blown up by the Royalist forces under MacLaine of Torloisk.

## Castle Sween

| | |
|---|---|
| *Location* | Castlesween, Kilmichael, Argyll. OS Map 62: NR 712788. |
| *Facilities* | None. |
| *Owner* | Historic Scotland. |
| *Tel* | 0131 668 8800. |
| *Open* | All year, Mon-Sun. |
| *Entry* | Free. |

Castle Sween is a magnificent building standing on a low headland that projects into Loch Sween. The irregular court is entered through a gateway in the south wall and remnants of buildings and a well can be seen inside. Three towers stand at corners of the yard, the south-east being the smallest, with a watch-chamber. The north-west contains the prison, and the north-east, or MacMillan's Tower, contains a fine kitchen range with an oven, millstone and querns. The oldest part of the castle was erected in the 12th century, but in the late 1400s it was improved and extended.

Tradition states that the castle was built by Sweyn, or Sueno, Prince of Denmark, in the 11th century, but certainly nothing of the present structure is as old. The MacSweens, or MacSuibhnes, held the fortress until after the Wars of Independence (1296-1314), having opposed Bruce. John MacSween tried unsuccessfully to recover the lands in 1311. The Lords of the Isles then obtained the castle,

which for some years was held by Hector MacNeill on their behalf.
In 1481 the castle returned to royal hands and James III placed it in
the keepership of Colin Campbell, Earl of Argyll. The building was
destroyed in 1647 when it was attacked by MacDonald of Colkitto.

## Duart Castle

| Location | Duart, Craignure, Island of Mull, PA64 6AP. |
| --- | --- |
| | OS Map 49: NM 749353. |
| Facilities | |
| Owner | Sir Lachlan Maclean, Bt. |
| Tel | 01680 812309. |
| Open | May-Oct, Mon-Sun. |
| Entry | ● |

Duart was built by the Macleans in the 13th century on a headland
guarding the Sound of Mull. It has mostly been in Maclean hands
ever since, though it was forfeited during the Jacobite uprising.
Ruinous since 1691, when it was taken by the Duke of Argyll, it was
restored to the plans of Sir John Burnet between 1910-12 by Sir
Fitzroy Maclean.

The great tower stands at the west corner of the courtyard, the
walls of which are up to 15ft-thick. The north and south sides have
17th-century buildings, but the south side is closed off with a wall
and gateway.

From the main gate the way is made into the ground floor of the
keep, where one sees the kitchen, scullery, 15ft-deep well and 'occupied' dungeons. One room has an exhibition on The Swan,
Cromwell's flagship, which sank off Duart in 1653. A spiral leads up

to the pantry, where there is a dumb waiter and dinner service. The Sea Room has windows overlooking the Sound of Mull, and contains relics of RMS Lochinvar. The Banqueting Hall has a large armorial fireplace, billiard table, and display cabinets with numerous artefacts. The stair leads up to the bedroom floor, where the State Bedroom and displays of clothing are shown. The top floor has exhibits on the restoration of the castle, the chiefs of Maclean, and Scouting – Lord Maclean being Chief Scout. The stair continues up to the battlements which afford wide views.

## Dunstaffnage Castle

| | |
|---|---|
| *Location* | Dunstaffnage, Dunbeg, Oban, Argyll. OS Map 49: NM 883344. |
| *Facilities* | |
| *Owner* | Historic Scotland. |
| *Tel* | 01631 562465. |
| *Open* | Apr-Sep, Mon-Sun. |
| *Entry* | |

Dunstaffnage is an impressive fortress comprising a curtain wall built on a solid rock boss. A steep stair and wooden platform lead to the entrance door, with a passageway into the courtyard. The gate-house dates from c.1500, and the upper floors were added c.1600. This block is still roofed, being restored in 1903, and the first floor hall contains a display on Argyll castles. The dormers were taken from a later house built in 1725, with the initials being of Angus and Lilias Campbell.

Two round towers are located at the north and west corners of the court, the western one containing a prison. The 1725 house is located between them. It has a large fireplace in the kitchen, and two decorative fire-surrounds on the floor (missing) above. In the courtyard is a large well, hewn from the solid rock. A modern stair leads to the wallhead, and the battlements afford views of the Firth of Lorn.

The MacDougalls built the original castle which dates from the 13th century. They were defeated in 1309 by Robert the Bruce and he granted the castle to the Campbells. The castle passed back to the MacDougalls, then to the Stewarts of Lorn and the Campbells again in 1470, who retained it until 1958 when it was taken into state care.

# 🏰 *Inveraray Castle*

| Location | Inveraray, Argyll, PA32 8XE. |
|---|---|
| | OS Map 56: NN 096092. |
| Facilities | 🏠🛈🎪🚻♿🍽 |
| Owner | Duke of Argyll. |
| Tel | 01499 302203. |
| Open | Apr-Jun, Sep-Oct, Sat-Thu; Jul-Aug, Mon-Sun. |
| Entry | ◓ |

Inveraray is a Gothic mansion of 1743-70, designed by Roger Morris. William and Robert Adam were also involved at a later date. The castle replaced an older baronial building which was demolished. Inveraray was altered in 1877-8 following a fire, when the candle-snuffer roofs were added to the corner turrets, and the central tower was raised in the middle of the four-square block. Often described as architecturally disappointing, the castle is nevertheless typical of its time.

The castle's interior outshines its exterior. Only one half of it is open to the public – the rooms on the north-west front. These are sumptuously furnished, with fine tapestries, paintings, furniture, china, wood carving and plasterwork, some of which was by Robert Adam. The armoury hall's walls are covered with guns and pikes. The

State Dining Room has exquisite painted panels on the walls and ceilings, which is the work of French artists. Other rooms include the saloon, gallery, Victorian room, drawing room, and MacArthur bedroom. One room is dedicated to the history and genealogy of the Campbell clan. The kitchen has a fine display of copper utensils.

Inveraray has been the seat of the Dukes of Argyll ever since it was built, and it is still lived in by the present Duke. The grounds are extensive, and contain the Combined Operations Museum.

## Kilchurn Castle

| | |
|---|---|
| *Location* | Loch Awe, Dalmally, Argyll. |
| | OS Map 50: NN 133276. |
| *Facilities* | None. |
| *Owner* | Historic Scotland. |
| *Tel* | 0131 668 8800. |
| *Open* | Apr-Sep, Mon-Sun. |
| *Entry* | Free. |

Kilchurn is well known from its regular appearance on calendars. A footpath from near the east end of the Orchy Bridge leads to the castle, built on a rock in the midst of what was an islet in the loch. Entry is made through the vaulted ground floor of the tower, the doorway having a lintel with the initials IEB and MCC, 1693 and Campbell arms on it. The tower dates from 1450. The castle was extended in 1693. Around 1550 the tower had turrets added to it; the inverted corbels of one lie in the courtyard.

A modern wooden stair leads to wooden platforms occupying the positions of the floors in the tower. A further stair leads to a viewing platform within a turret, which has little shot holes. There are large corbels which formerly supported a wooden floor. At the southern end of the courtyard is a small round tower, with dumbell gunloops. Another round tower is located at the northern corner, with a garderobe off it. Near it is a water inlet chute.

Kilchurn was built by the Campbells, John, 1st Earl of Breadalbane making the 17th-century additions. The castle was used as a garrison during the 1745 rebellion and de-roofed in 1770. It was taken into state care in 1953.

## 🏠 *Rothesay Castle*

| | |
|---|---|
| *Location* | Rothesay, Isle of Bute. OS Map 63: NS 088647. |
| *Facilities* | 🏠 ♨ ♿ ♿ |
| *Owner* | Historic Scotland. |
| *Tel* | 01700 502691. |
| *Open* | Apr-Sep, Mon-Sun; Oct-Mar, Sat-Thur. |
| *Entry* | ↻ |

Located in the centre of Rothesay, this circular-plan castle of enclosure still stands in its moat, and is one of Scotland's oldest castles. Entry is made over a wooden bridge to the Forework, which is a vaulted passage over which is the great hall. A ladder descends to the pit prison, which has a tiny window overlooking the moat. The original entrance is located nearer the centre of the castle. Two stairs lead up to the 16th-century great hall, restored in 1900 by the 3rd Marquess of Bute – the red sandstone indicates new work. This attractive hall has a large fireplace and displays.

The circular wall round the courtyard formerly had four round towers, and only the doocot tower has survived to any great extent. The pigeon holes are still visible at its upper level. Remains of the Chapel Royal of St Michael are located at the east side of the courtyard, and are adorned with a modern wooden cross and plaque in memory of the 6th Marquess of Bute. The lower floor was a store, and the upper was the chapel, with a piscina and remnants of window tracery. A well survives in the courtyard.

Rothesay was built in the 13th century by the Stewart kings, though it is claimed a castle stood here in 1098. It was captured by Vikings in 1230. Robert III died here in 1406. The gate-house was completed in 1541. The castle was destroyed in 1685 during Argyll's Rebellion. The 3rd Marquess of Bute commenced restoration work in the late-19th century, commissioning William Burges to provide a plan. The castle was placed in state care in 1961, though the Marquess remains Hereditary Keeper.

## Skipness Castle

| | |
|---|---|
| *Location* | Skipness, Tarbert, Argyll. |
| | OS Map 62: NR 908577. |
| *Facilities* | None. |
| *Owner* | Historic Scotland. |
| *Tel* | 0131 668 8800. |
| *Open* | All Year, Mon-Sun. |
| *Entry* | Free. |

Skipness today is like a square tower house with a walled courtyard to the south-west of it. However, the castle has a complicated history, as it was extended over the years. Only fragments of the ancient hall survive in the north wall of the courtyard, through which a gateway was made when the castle became a farm. The south wall has ornate window openings at an upper level, indicating that the 13th-century chapel stood here. This was altered in the early-14th century when the two buildings were linked by the great courtyard wall, an impressive gatehouse formed in the south wall. A new Kilbrannan Chapel was erected nearby. The north-west latrine tower doubled as a doocot. The north-east tower dates from the 16th century, and has the distinctive red sandstone dressings like the rest of the castle. The ground floor of this tower is vaulted, the first floor entrance reached by later steps.

Skipness was probably built by the MacDonald Lords of the Isles but in 1493 ownership passed to the Campbells. In 1898 the farm buildings were removed by the laird and the process of restoration commenced.

## ![icon] Torosay Castle

| | |
|---|---|
| *Location* | Craignure, Island of Mull, PA65 6AY. |
| | OS Map 49: NM 729353. |
| *Facilities* | ▢ ▲ ⊞ ♨ ✕ ὰ |
| *Owner* | Christopher James. |
| *Tel* | 01680 812421. |
| *Open* | Apr-Oct, Mon-Sun. |
| *Entry* | ◖ |

Torosay Castle is really just a Victorian baronial mansion, dating from 1858 and designed by David Bryce. Originally known as Duart House, it was renamed Torosay when Duart Castle was restored. It was built for John Campbell but the expense forced him to sell in 1865. It was purchased by the Guthrie family, whose descendants, later Guthrie-James, still own it.

Tours take one through the entrance hall, with sporting trophies and taxidermy, to the central hall. The sitting room is followed by the attractive dining room, which overlooks the garden on two sides. The library is filled with books old and new. The Yellow Drawing Room contains a large painting of the family by Frederick Whiting. The 'Viking' room is dedicated to the four-masted barque of that name which journeyed round the world in 1937-8. The archive room contains relics associated with David James, a noted explorer and prisoner-of-war, who wrote a number of books. A lesser stair leads up to a bedroom with a nursery above it. A small exhibition on Winston Churchill notes his association with the castle. Torosay has a fine selection of portraits, paintings, World War I militaria and shipping collections.

Torosay is a family castle, and visitors are invited to make themselves at home. The information notices are often humorous. The gardens extend to 12 acres and include a statue walk, various terraces, and the Japanese garden. A narrow gauge railway can be used to reach the castle from near Craignure pier.

# The Borders

*Aikwood Tower*

| | |
|---|---|
| *Location* | Oakwood, Ettrickdale, Selkirk, TD7 5HJ. OS Map 73: NT 419260. |
| *Facilities* | |
| *Owner* | Lord Steel of Aikwood. |
| *Tel* | 01750 52253. |
| *Open* | May-Sep, Tue, Thu, Sun. |
| *Entry* | |

Aikwood, sometimes spelled Oakwood, was restored between1990 and 1992 by Sir David Steel, the last leader of the Liberal Party. The old byre adjoining the castle plays host to exhibitions which are changed regularly. Currently artefacts of the Border writer James Hogg are on display and include first editions, his spectacles, seal, fiddle, and a letter to his wife regarding his possible knighthood. Stairs lead to the loft, converted into a working study for the Steels. Entry is then made to the tower's great hall, which has a fine joggled lintel over the fireplace, bearing mason's marks. A number of small aumbries survive. To one side is the laird's room, with mementos of Sir David's time as an MP. A left-handed spiral stair leads down to the vaulted vestibule, with a view through the hatch to the vaulted kitchen. From here is a doorway to the garden. Tours return to the byre.

The lands of Aikwood were granted to Michael Scott by James V in 1517, though the tower may not have been erected until around 1535. A datestone commemorates the marriage of Robert Scott in 1602. The tower passed to the Murrays and then back to the Scotts, and remained in their hands until purchased by the Duke of

Buccleuch in the 1940s. The tower had long been abandoned, however, and was converted for agricultural use.

Externally the tower is very fine, with sheer walls rising to an ornate corbel course, decorated with saltires. The tower rises to four storeys plus an attic, the corner cap-houses being distinctive roof-line features.

# 🏰 *Ayton Castle*

| | |
|---|---|
| *Location* | Ayton, Eyemouth, Berwickshire, TD14 5RD. OS Map 67: NT 929614. |
| *Facilities* | ♿ ☕ |
| *Owner* | David I Liddell-Grainger. |
| *Tel* | 018907 81212/81550. |
| *Open* | May-Sep, Sun. |
| *Entry* | ℗ |

Ayton is a grand neo-baronial red sandstone castle, built between 1845 and 1848 for William Mitchell-Innes, to the plans of James Gillespie-Graham. It is a confection of turrets, towers, water-spouts and corbie-stepped gables. The main tower rises to four and a half storeys. Tradition states that the castle was built without a plan, and that the client instructed the masons to add bits as he felt they were required, but this is known to be false. Mitchell-Innes's son, Alexander, inherited the castle and added to it. When he died in 1886 the castle was sold to Henry Liddell, whose descendants still own it, though it was used for a time as a girls' school.

Guided tours commence at the carriage entry. The tour shows a series of first floor bedrooms and then descends the large spiral staircase to the library and the wainscoted L-shaped drawing room. The main hall is a fine L-shaped apartment, with a dining area in one branch. It has armorial plasterwork on the ceiling.

The dining room proper has a large bay window overlooking the Eye valley, and has silver polo trophies, African statuettes, 17th-century mirrors, and a replica fireplace – the original was removed and sold to the American author, Mark Twain, who had fallen in love with it.

##  *Drumlanrig's Tower*

| | |
|---|---|
| *Location* | 1 Towerknowe, Hawick, TD9 9EN. |
| | OS Map 79: NT 502144. |
| *Facilities* | ⌖ ♿ ☕ |
| *Owner* | Borders Council. |
| *Tel* | 01450 373457. |
| *Open* | All Year, Mon-Sun. |
| *Entry* | ◔ |

Drumlanrig's Tower is quite a unique towerhouse regarding its location and history. Situated in the heart of Hawick, it was for many years part of the Tower Hotel until it closed in the 1970s. The building was restored in the 1990s and opened in 1995 as a tourist and interpretive centre.

The 'Black Tower of Drumlanrig' was erected in the 16th century by William Douglas, as an L-planned building with a small courtyard walled off in the re-entrant. It rose three storeys in height with a spiral stair in the wing. In the 18th century the tower was extended as a town-house residence of Anne, Duchess of Monmouth and Buccleuch. By around 1773 it had been converted to the main inn in the town, visited on 22nd September 1803 by Sir Walter Scott, and William and Dorothy Wordsworth.

From the tourist information centre one enters the ground floor of the tower which is vaulted and still has gunloops. A spiral stair leads to the former great hall, with a large fireplace and modern painted ceiling. Above again were the private chambers. A doorway on the 3rd floor leads to the parapet walk. To see the tower externally one has to view it from the rear, the street side being lost in the later additions.

The tower is the location for exhibitions on the history of the Border country, the subjects of which go from Romans to knitwear, reivers and local history. There is also an exhibition of watercolours by the artist Tom Scott.

## Floors Castle

| Location | Kelso, Roxburghshire, TD5 7SF. |
| --- | --- |
| | OS Map 74: NT 711347. |
| Facilities | ▢▲⊞♿♨✕♨ |
| Owner | Duke of Roxburghe. |
| Tel | 01573 223333. |
| Open | Easter-Sep, Mon-Sun; Oct, Sun, Wed. |
| Entry | ◖ |

The 1st Duke of Roxburghe employed William Adam to design the present large mansion (the largest in Scotland) which was erected between 1721-26. In 1837-47, William Playfair made alterations to the building, leaving it with a more romantic roofscape. The central block rises four storeys in height, with five in the towers, and is built of random rubble. The roof line sports ornamental turrets and corbel courses. The large wings rise to three storeys in places and echo the central block in style.

Entry is made from the fine porte-cochere up stairs to the entrance hall, which is adorned with paintings. The smaller ante-room is followed by the more ornate sitting room. The large drawing room has Belgian tapestries and fine furnishings. The Needle Room is located in a corner turret. The ballroom is a fine apartment, and was added by Playfair in 1842. It was altered in the early 20th century, when the American oak panelling and Grinling Gibbons-type carvings were added. Passages, with plans of the alterations on display, lead to the many other rooms: the Bird Room with taxidermy, geological and numismatic (coin) specimens; the billiard room, with large portraits, and the gallery and dining rooms.

The castle has innumerable examples of fine furnishings, paintings, gold plate, marble figures and porcelain. In the basement area are collections of small artefacts including china, guns, fishing, ephemera and an icing-sugar model of the castle.

## Greenknowe Tower

| | |
|---|---|
| *Location* | Earlston Road, Gordon, Berwickshire. OS Map 74: NT 639428. |
| *Facilities* | |
| *Owner* | Historic Scotland. |
| *Tel* | 0131 668 8800. |
| *Open* | All Year, Mon-Sun. |
| *Entry* | Free. |

The green knoll on which this castle was built is not very high, but was formerly surrounded by the extensive Gordon Moss which would have improved its defensive position. The tower, which is constructed in a dark whinstone with sandstone quoins and other dressings, was erected in 1581 by James Seton of Touch and Janet Edmonstone, whose arms appear over the door. A fine yett leads to the base of the east wing. Off to the left is the vaulted kitchen which has a gunloop, slop chute and ceiling meat-hooks. A wide newel stair leads to the first floor hall which has a large fireplace and laird's lug adjacent. A lesser stairway in the re-entrant leads on up to the top of the tower, but all the floors are now gone, save for a modern one at the top floor of the wing. The rooms over the hall have fine fireplaces and windows.

Externally Greenknowe is distinguished by its string course on the wing, corbelled bartizans, and corbie-stepped gables. In the grounds are the remnants of a stable.

In the late-17th century Greenknowe was owned by Walter Pringle of Stichel, a noted writer and Covenanter. The tower remained occupied until about 1850. In 1937 it was passed into state care by the Dalrymple family, and they gave a donation towards its consolidation through the Dalrymple Archaeological Trust.

## ⌂ *Hermitage Castle*

| | |
|---|---|
| *Location* | Hermitage, Newcastleton, Roxburghshire. |
| | OS Map 79: NY 496960. |
| *Facilities* | ⌷ ᵹ̇ |
| *Owner* | Historic Scotland. |
| *Tel* | 013873 376222. |
| *Open* | Apr-Sep, Mon-Sun. |
| *Entry* | ➊ |

Hermitage is a very fine and sizeable castle of the 14th and 15th centuries, and stands by the side of the Hermitage Water. The low arched doorway leads to the courtyard, at one time the centre of a 14th-century tower house. This was greatly extended in the late 14th and 15th centuries to form the present elaborate plan, with four towers at the corners and the great oversailing arches between them on the west and east facades. The corbelling is particularly fine, and over the doorway is a machicolation.

The east range contains the pit and the prison which was converted into a gun-port in the 16th century. The north-west tower formerly had wooden floors but these have long since gone. A modern steel stairway gives partial access. The topmost room of the tower still retains its vaulted ceiling, however. The south-west tower contains the kitchen, with quern, fireplaces, oven and a drain to an external cesspool. Above it is a unique corner fireplace. Between these two towers was the original entrance, now blocked, but on one wall the slits for two portcullises can still be seen. The top two storeys of the south west tower have more ornate windows.

The oldest surviving part of the castle was probably erected around 1350 by the Dacre family using English masons. The castle soon passed to the Douglases, who remained until 1492, creating what we see today. In 1491 James IV ordered them to surrender the castle to the Hepburns of Bothwell, with the Douglases receiving Bothwell Castle in exchange. In 1540 the castle was taken over by the Crown, though the Hepburns still held it. Mary, Queen of Scots visited the Earl of Bothwell here on 15 October 1566. The castle was acquired by the Scotts around 1600, but was then abandoned. The Duke of Buccleuch made some restorations in 1820 and it passed into care in 1930.

## Neidpath Castle

| | |
|---|---|
| *Location* | Peebles, Peeblesshire, EH45 8NW. |
| | OS Map 73: NT 236404. |
| *Facilities* | |
| *Owner* | Lady Elizabeth Benson. |
| *Tel* | 01721 720333. |
| *Open* | Easter-Sep, Mon-Sun. |
| *Entry* | |

Romantically situated on a bend of the River Tweed, just one mile west of Peebles, Neidpath is a well-known castle by sight. The tower was erected around 1370 by the Hays. This family later became Lords Hay of Yester and then Earls of Tweeddale. In 1686 the estate was sold to the Douglas Dukes of Queensberry, one of whom allowed the castle to become neglected. In 1810 the castle passed to the Earl of Wemyss, whose heir is styled Lord Neidpath.

The present entrance door dates from the 17th century and leads to the vaulted laigh hall. Here are displays of artefacts found during excavation (including a mummified rat!), tartans, and relics associated with the castle and owners.

In the west wing is the prison and pit, now entered from a later opening. Also on this lower floor is 21ft-deep well, the original entrance and carved stones. The spiral staircase can be taken back up to the first floor to the great hall which is panelled in timber. In the 'Chalmer' or private room, there is a huge fireplace with mason's marks. A modern W.C. has an aumbry and views of the Tweed. In the west wing was the kitchen, most of which has collapsed but which was excavated in 1992. To the north-west is a private turnpike to the second floor and battlements. The second floor has two bedrooms, one styled as Queen Mary's Room, for Mary, Queen of Scots stayed in 1563, but not in this room. James VI stayed in 1587. The third floor has lesser bedrooms, one with fragments of painted beams. A lintel in the south-west turnpike has a carved sword on it, indicating that it was once a mediaeval gravestone. Two wall walks afford impressive views. The present roof dates from 1938. The courtyard has a modern cottage and ruins of a bakehouse, plus an ornate gateway with the Hay crest on a keystone.

# ⌂ *Smailholm Tower*

| | |
|---|---|
| *Location* | Sandyknowe, Smailholm, Roxburghshire. |
| | OS Map 74: NT 638346. |
| *Facilities* | ⬛ ⚘ |
| *Owner* | Historic Scotland. |
| *Tel* | 01573 460365. |
| *Open* | Apr-Sep, Mon-Sun. |
| *Entry* | ⚲ |

Smailholm Tower is an impressive structure famed in Border ballad and associated with Sir Walter Scott, who spent some of his childhood recuperating at Sandyknowe Farm in 1773. A sturdy rectangular tower, built of rubble with sandstone dressings, it perches on a rock outcrop. The rock had a barmkin wall around it, and ruins of lesser buildings exist within this – old kitchens and halls. The gateway is at the west end, with its dressed stones long-since robbed.

The tower, however, is virtually complete, apart from its roof slabs, though the supporting vault survives. The entrance is through a door in the south wall, leading to a vault. Within it is a modern timber floor reached by a spiral stair. Within the south-west corner of the tower a newel stair leads up through the floors. The first was the great hall, with window benches, fireplace, aumbries and latrine. The second floor is similar in style, though less decorative. The third floor is vaulted and doors lead out to the two viewing parapets which afford wide panoramas.

The tower contains dressed models by Anne Carrick depicting Scott's *Minstrelsy of the Scottish Borders*, tapestries and paintings. There are also models of the tower, and relics found during the excavations of the courtyard buildings in 1979-81. Smailholm was built by the Pringles around the middle of the 15th century but passed into Scott hands in 1645. A few years after 1700 it was abandoned in favour of Sandyknowe. The castle was often raided by the English in the 1540s.

## ♟ *Thirlestane Castle*

| | |
|---|---|
| *Location* | Lauder, Berwickshire, TD2 6RU.<br>OS Map 73: NT 533479. |
| *Facilities* | ▢▲⊞ₐ ♨ ⅍ |
| *Owner* | Thirlestane Castle Trust/Gerald Maitland-Carew. |
| *Tel* | 01578 722430 |
| *Open* | Easter; May-Jun, Sep, Mon, Wed-Thu, Sun; Jul-Aug, Sun-Fri. |
| *Entry* | ● |

One of the finest castles in Scotland, Thirlestane is a confection of turrets, dormers and balustrades with random rubble walls dressed with sandstone. The oldest part of the castle dates from 1590, but it was remodelled in the 1670s and 1840s, creating a T-shaped pile. The castle has always been the property of the Maitland family, including the Earls of Lauderdale. It was placed in the care of the Trust in 1984.

Tours of the castle commence at the main entrance, which leads into the hall, where there is a model of the castle, a granite fireplace and wainscoting. The Panelled Room is followed by the main library, formerly a dining room, now with 18th-century books along two walls. The billiard room has another granite fireplace, where the firescreen is a collection of fishing flies. On show are old photographs taken by the 14th Earl who was a pioneer photographer. One corner turret contains more photographic collections. The other turret contains a lesser library, from where a spiral stair (one of eleven in the castle – this being the only left-handed one) leads up to the Duke's Room. The Red Drawing Room and Bonnie Prince Charlie's bedroom follow (he stayed in November 1745). The Large Drawing Room comprises two former rooms which were joined in the 1840 alterations. The next suite of rooms include the dining room, Chinese Room and Maitland Room, which has family memorabilia. The nurseries have a fine display of toys. A stair descends to the country life exhibitions of taxidermy, country trades, tailor's shop and other exhibits.

# Dumfries
and Galloway

# 🏠 *Caerlaverock Castle*

| | |
|---|---|
| *Location* | Greenhead, Caerlaverock, Dumfries. |
| | OS Map 84: NY 025656. |
| *Facilities* | 🏠 🍴 ♿ ♿ ♿ |
| *Owner* | Historic Scotland. |
| *Tel* | 01387 770244. |
| *Open* | All Year, Mon-Sun. |
| *Entry* | ☛ |

This great red sandstone castle stands surrounded by a protective moat. Triangular in plan, it has round towers at the 'rear' corners, and a double tower at the apex entrance. On crossing the drawbridge the portcullis gate is passed and the inner courtyard reached. On the east side of this rises the magnificent Nithsdale Apartments, built in 1634 with a decorative Renaissance front. Ornate pediments with arms and other symbols are located over each window. Within one of the vaults is the old well. The western range of building dates from the 15th century, at the south-east corner of which is Murdoch's Tower. Though the castle is ruinous, most rooms can be visualised, and many of them have ornate fire-surrounds.

Caerlaverock was built around 1270 by Sir Herbert Maxwell. In 1300 it was placed under siege by Edward I of England, with three thousand men. The garrison's sixty men held out for two days. The castle suffered further attacks in 1312, 1356, 1545, 1570 and in 1640 for thirteen weeks. After each siege, except the last, the castle was rebuilt.

The castle remained in Maxwell ownership until it passed to the Dukes of Norfolk, who placed it in guardianship in 1946. In the grounds are a children's playground, cannon and rebuilt mangonel.

 *Cardoness Castle*

| | |
|---|---|
| *Location* | Gatehouse of Fleet, Kirkcudbrightshire. OS Map 83: NX 591553. |
| *Facilities* | ▢ |
| *Owner* | Historic Scotland. |
| *Tel* | 01557 814427. |
| *Open* | Apr-Sep, Mon-Sun; Oct-Mar, Sat-Sun. |
| *Entry* | ☞ |

Cardoness is a tall square tower standing on a low hillock to the west of Gatehouse. Lower vaulted cellars are located below the tower to the south, and a ramp leads to the entrance doorway. This leads into the vaulted cellar, which contains two girnals and a slop chute. To the left of the door is a guard room and over the vestibule is a murder hole from where intruders could be shot. A stair ascends to the great hall, which has an attractive fireplace. To either side of this are a buffet (with ornate ogee moulding) and a salt box.

Off the stair is the prison with pit below. The stair continues up to the third floor (now missing) but it can be approached from the passage. Up at parapet level is an impressive viewpoint.

Cardoness was built in the late-15th century by the MacCullochs. Alexander MacCulloch, laird between 1509-13, was keeper of James IV's falcon and won 35 shillings at archery butts.

The estate was acquired by the Gordons in 1629, but the MacCullochs did not like this. In 1668 Alexander MacCulloch disputed with the Gordons, and caused the death of a sick widow. In 1697 Sir Godfrey MacCulloch was executed by 'The Maiden' in Edinburgh. The castle has been empty since then.

## Carsluith Castle

| | |
|---|---|
| *Location* | Carsluith, Creetown, Kirkcudbrightshire. OS Map 83: NX 494541. |
| *Facilities* | None. |
| *Owner* | Historic Scotland. |
| *Tel* | 0131 668 8800. |
| *Open* | All Year, Mon-Sun. |
| *Entry* | Free. |

This is a small and attractive tower-house, situated in the middle of a farmstead. It dates from the 16th century, with an addition in 1568 built by Richard Brown, whose worn arms are above the doorway. L-shaped in plan, the spiral stair in the projection leads up to the great hall. Adjacent to the fireplace is a small salt box. A stone slop-sink empties through a grotesque gargoyle on the outside wall.

Two vaulted cellars are located beneath the hall. There was no kitchen in the castle; this would have been located outwith the main tower as a fire precaution. A lesser stair climbs to the upper floors, now gone, which affords views of the wall-head, where the stone slabs and water-spouts can easily be seen and appreciated. A small chamber over the main stair is also reached by this second stair, as was an unusual wooden balcony hanging over the entrance, which is now also gone. In 1579 John Brown was implicated in the murder of MacCulloch of Barholm. Gilbert Brown was the last abbot of Sweetheart, and a staunch Catholic. He was imprisoned at Blackness Castle in 1605, but James VI released him and he died in France in 1612. The last of the Browns of Carsluith emigrated to India in 1748, when the castle was abandoned.

## Castle of St John

| | |
|---|---|
| *Location* | Castle Street, Stranraer, Wigtownshire. |
| | OS Map 82: NX 060618. |
| *Facilities* | 📖 |
| *Owner* | Dumfries & Galloway Council. |
| *Tel* | 01776 705544. |
| *Open* | Apr-Sep, Mon-Sat. |
| *Entry* | ☞ |

Known also as Chapel or Stranraer Castle, this tall tower stands in the middle of the town. Built of grey stone, it has sandstone dressings. It is four storeys tall, with each floor vaulted, and a turnpike in a projection leads to them all. A worn panel is over the doorway.

The ground floor has two vaulted cellars, which formerly had entresols. The first floor was the great hall, with a large fireplace. There is a display of Covenanting banners, and a video on the years of the Covenant, as the castle acted as a garrison then. A guard room is located over the entrance – the pit may still be seen in the thickness of the walls. The second and third floor were both converted to prison cells, the castle being the town gaol from 1815 until 1907. The debtors' cells are slightly more comfortable. The stair continues up to the battlements, with a viewpoint over Loch Ryan, flagstaff and a bell tower dated 1853.

The castle was built by Ninian Adair in 1510 and passed to the Kennedys by 1595. The Dalrymples of Stair bought it in 1680. It was acquired by the Burgh of Stranraer in 1815 for £340. Latterly used as a store and meeting place, it was restored by the former Wigtown District Council and opened to the public in 1990.

 ## *Drumcoltran Tower*

| | |
|---|---|
| *Location* | Drumcoltran, Kirkgunzeon, Kirkcudbrightshire. OS Map 84: NX 869683. |
| *Facilities* | None. |
| *Owner* | Historic Scotland. |
| *Tel* | 0131 668 8800. |
| *Open* | All year, Mon-Sun. |
| *Entry* | Free. |

This is an attractive small rubble-built house, located in the middle of a farm steading. L-shaped in plan, the doorway is in the re-entrant and a wide spiral stair leads to the hall on the first floor. Beneath this is a vaulted kitchen with a large fireplace, which was originally located in the great hall. The two fireplaces now in the hall are of recent origin. The stair continues up to the cap-house, which is still a cosy little room with a fireplace and a small window.

A doorway leads out to the battlements, which have red sandstone flags. Drainage holes lead through gargoyles. The view over the farmstead and surrounding hillocks is charming. The turret in the re-entrant formerly had a conical roof.

Drumcoltran was built around 1550 for the Maxwell family, with Sir John Maxwell marrying the Herries heiress. A Latin motto over the door translates as 'Conceal secrets, be timid of speech, be truthful, beware of wine, remember death, be pitiful.' The panel which would have borne arms and a date is missing.

In 1669 the tower was sold to the Irvings, followed by the Hynds in 1799, the Herons, and the Maxwells again in 1875. It was still inhabited in the 1890s.

## Drumlanrig Castle

| Location | Thornhill, Dumfriesshire, DG3 4AQ. |
| | OS Map 78: NX 852992. |
| *Facilities* | 📷 ▲ ♨ ⚓ ♿ 🎪 |
| *Owner* | Duke of Buccleuch. |
| *Tel* | 01848 330248. |
| *Open* | May-Aug, Fri-Wed. |
| *Entry* | ● |

A vast pink sandstone mansion, Drumlanrig is a transition between the traditional castle and the country house. It has four towers, many turrets and spiral stairs. It was built between 1679-91 for the 1st Duke of Queensberry (Douglas) who was so incensed at the cost that he spent only one night within it, preferring 15th-century Sanquhar Castle.

Tours begin in the west wing. They reach the entrance hall where arched windows overlook the courtyard with its traditional iron yett. The inner hall contains a collection of arms, militaria and games. The east passage leads to the stair hall, with a grand staircase. The morning room contains a modern painting of the 9th Duchess. The dining room has wood carvings on the panelling, barometers and silver candlestands. A spiral stair leads to Prince Charlie's bedroom, and contains a few Jacobite relics. The drawing room is sumptuously furnished, with full-length portraits. The castle has many notable paintings, by artists like da Vinci, Rembrandt and Holbein, and numerous antique furnishings, many of which date from the 17th century.

Drumlanrig's grounds contain a country park, formal gardens, craft workshops, a cycle museum and numerous walks.

## Lochmaben Castle

| | |
|---|---|
| *Location* | Castle Mains, Lochmaben, Dumfriesshire. OS Map 78: NY 088812. |
| *Facilities* | &#9855; |
| *Owner* | Historic Scotland. |
| *Tel* | 0131 668 8800. |
| *Open* | All Year, Mon-Sun. |
| *Entry* | Free. |

Lochmaben Castle stands on a low headland projecting into the Castle Loch, a spot which formerly was an island. The ruins are extensive, but most of the dressed sandstone has been robbed over the years, leaving only crumbling rubble. To the south the walls reach their highest, with a great entrance over a ditch. The drawbridge pit is still visible. Arches cross over the ditch to form what was one of the most unusual foreworks in Scotland. North of this are lesser buildings, now much ruinous, but two vaulted rooms are discernible, as well as a number of outbuildings. There are two great chunks of fallen masonry. South of the present moat, which would have allowed access by boat, there was probably a large courtyard with a timber wall surrounded by another ditch.

What we see of Lochmaben was probably built by English masons, and in its early years it was captured and recaptured 12 times, being close to the border. Originally the seat of the Bruces, some say King Robert was born here, though others claim this for Turnberry Castle in Ayrshire. Edward I of England took the castle in 1298, but it returned to Bruce hands. It was given to Edward III by Baliol but taken again by David II in 1346. Edward captured it again, but the Douglases retook it in 1384. When the Douglases were attaint in 1455 it became a royal castle. James IV did much rebuilding in 1503-4, adding a new hall. Mary, Queen of Scots visited in 1565 with Darnley. For a time held by Lord Maxwell, it was besieged in 1588 by James VI who granted the governorship to the Earls of Annandale.

## MacLellan's Castle

| | |
|---|---|
| *Location* | Kirkcudbright. |
| | OS Maps 83, 84: NX 683511. |
| *Facilities* | |
| *Owner* | Historic Scotland. |
| *Tel* | 01557 331856. |
| *Open* | Apr-Sep, Mon-Sun. |
| *Entry* | |

This large town house was built in 1582 by Sir Thomas MacLellan of Bombie, Provost of Kirkcudbright. Tradition states that some of the fifteen rooms in the upper three floors were never completed. The MacLellans, created Lords Kirkcudbright in 1633, fell upon hard times and by 1664 most of the estates were sold. The castle was abandoned by 1700 and the roof stripped in 1752. It was taken into state care in 1912.

The castle has an elaborate L-plan. The entrance is in the main re-entrant. The well is located outwith this. There are five vaulted rooms on the ground floor, with that to the west being the kitchen, complete with serving hatch, slop drain and bread oven. There are a few gunloops through the walls.

The stair leads to the first floor, where the great hall has a huge lintel over the fireplace. The laird's chamber is beyond this. Two lesser chambers are located in the wings, and each has a latrine. From the stair hall is a small room which overlooks the entrance. Also from here is a small aperture through to the great hall fireplace – the laird's lug. There were three newel staircases leading to the upper floors, which are now gone, but the walls are basically complete to the eaves.

## Morton Castle

| | |
|---|---|
| *Location* | Morton Mains, Carronbridge, Thornhill, Dumfriesshire. OS Map 78: NX 891992. |
| *Facilities* | None. |
| *Owner* | Duke of Buccleuch/Historic Scotland. |
| *Tel* | 0131 668 8800. |
| *Open* | All Year, Mon-Sun. |
| *Entry* | Free. |

Morton Castle stands on a headland above a small loch at the foot of the Lowther Hills. It is a massive hall-type castle and much of the work dates from the late-13th century. A pathway leads to the entrance gateway, only one tower of which survives, but the dressed stones where the drawbridge mechanism would have been remains. To the right is the main hall, now missing its floors. In the gate tower is a prison pit. Above it the remains of a small stairway lead from the first to second floor. The ground floor of the main block has seven small windows on the south wall, two slop-chutes and a fireplace.

The hall above had larger windows, the stone mullions of which have partially survived, although the grilles are gone. This hall had a timber floor and ceiling, and measured 93ft by 31ft. The south-east tower, which is half-demolished, had a private room within it and latrines in the thickness of the walls. These emptied into a large chute which cuts across the neck of the tower. The north wall has corbels which would have supported a lean-to roof (west end) and a floor (east end). A first-floor doorway here has an ornate pointed arch moulding.

Morton Castle was the principal seat of the Douglas Earls of Morton and seems to have remained in occupation until the beginning of the 18th century. The castle was probably erected around 1370 when James Douglas was confirmed by the king as owner.

## 🏠 *Orchardton Tower*

| | |
|---|---|
| *Location* | Old Orchardton, Palnackie, Kirkcudbrightshire. OS Map 84: NX 817551. |
| *Facilities* | None. |
| *Owner* | Historic Scotland. |
| *Tel* | 0131 668 8800. |
| *Open* | All year, Mon-Sat. |
| *Entry* | Free. |

Orchardton is unique in Scotland, being the only example of a cylindrical tower-house. It is solidly built of granite, and the rock foundations are bared at one point. On the ground floor is a vaulted cellar, entered through an arched doorway. An external stairway leads to the first floor. The present door was originally a window, with the original entrance being rather low. Within this chamber is a decorative aumbry or laver and carved stone, both thought to have been taken from an abandoned abbey like Tongland or Dundrennan. This room may have been converted into a private chapel. The great hall was located over the ruins to the east.

A tiny spiral stair, with treads two feet wide, leads up to the little cap-house and the airy battlements. These have overlapping flag-stones. Off the stair is a garderobe. To the east one can view the associated ruins, a vault, rooms, slop-sink and the original stairway to the entrance.

Orchardton was built for John Carnys (Cairns) around 1456. Ownership passed through an heiress in 1633 to the Maxwells, the most famous of which was Sir Robert Maxwell, an ardent Jacobite who was captured at Culloden. He is featured in Scott's *Guy Mannering*.

## Threave Castle

| | |
|---|---|
| *Location* | Kelton Mains, Castle Douglas, Kirkcudbright. OS Maps 83, 84: NX 739623. |
| *Facilities* | |
| *Owner* | National Trust for Scotland/Historic Scotland. |
| *Tel* | 01831 168512. |
| *Open* | Apr-Sep, Mon-Sun. |
| *Entry* | |

From the car park visitors should follow the path to the ferry across the River Dee to Threave Island. If the river conditions are such that the ferry cannot sail, then a notice is left at the car park.

Threave was built around 1369 by Sir Archibald Douglas to help pacify Galloway. However, he became a threat himself. The Black Douglas was overthrown in 1455 and the Crown appointed keepers until 1526 when the Maxwells became hereditary keepers. The castle was attacked by the Covenanters in 1640 after which it was abandoned. For a short time it acted as a prison during the French wars. It was placed in state care in 1913 by Edward Gordon, and given to the National Trust in 1948 by Major A.F. Gordon.

A drawbridge crosses the moat to the artillery fortification, which was built around 1450 when James II was expected to attack from this side. He actually attacked from the west, where there is a small harbour. A wooden stair leads to the doorway. Internally the floor has gone, but one can imagine the line of this, with the prison, well and cellar below, and vaulted kitchen above. A model of the 1455 siege and a Douglas banner are on display. A spiral stair leads up to the great hall, which has a flagged floor. The floors above are ruinous.

# Dundee
# and Angus

*Broughty Castle*

| | |
|---|---|
| *Location* | Broughty Ferry, Dundee, Angus. |
| | OS Map 54: NO 465304. |
| *Facilities* | None. |
| *Owner* | Historic Scotland/City of Dundee Council. |
| *Tel* | 01382 76121 |
| *Open* | All Year, Mon-Sun. |
| *Entry* | Free. |

Built to guard the Firth of Tay, Broughty Castle looks today to be a fine tower house which dates c.1454, when the 4th Earl of Angus was granted permission by James II to erect one. However, the upper walls of the tower, as well as the present stair turret, date from 1860-1, and were built when the country feared an attack from France. The restorations were designed by Robert Rowand Anderson.

A drawbridge (with large chain and weights) over the dry ditch leads into the courtyard, the walls of which date from the 1860s. The castle is entered at the foot of the main tower, and a stair leads to the first floor. The lower vaults are not open to the public. The rooms in the castle are now used for museum exhibits, displaying examples of militaria, whaling, fishing, lifeboats, railways, ferries, sea-life and local history. The 4th floor has a small observation room, added in 1942.

Broughty passed to the Gray family in the 1490s, who remained owners until 1666. The Fothringhams then acquired it, but in 1787 Robert Burns noted it was a ruin. The castle was subject to an attack in 1547, though it surrendered without firing a shot in anger. It remained in English hands until 1560 when it surrendered to a

Franco-Scots army. In modern times the castle has been a garrison for various regiments, being armed with guns during both World Wars. It was converted into a museum in 1969.

# Edzell Castle

| | |
|---|---|
| *Location* | Edzell, Brechin, Angus. |
| | OS Map 44: NO 584692. |
| *Facilities* | ⌂ ♠ ⚑ ⚹ ⚐ |
| *Owner* | Historic Scotland. |
| *Tel* | 01356 648631. |
| *Open* | Apr-Sep, Mon-Sun; Oct-Mar, Sat-Thu. |
| *Entry* | ⊙ |

It is actually the garden at Edzell which seems to be more important than the castle itself. It has a large enclosed area, and the walls are adorned with numerous carvings of Planetary Deities, Liberal Arts and Cardinal Virtues. These are actually now resin casts of the originals, which are located in the delectable Summer House of 1604. The garden dates from this time, being laid out by Sir David Lindsay, Lord Edzell, but the present parterre was the work of the Ancient Monuments Board in 1932 when the garden was taken into state care. At the opposite corner of the garden from the summer house are the scanty remains of the bath house, with the well surviving in the thickness of the wall.

The oldest part of the castle is the L-planned tower of the early-16th century, which is built in a rich red sandstone. This was added to on the north where the entrance pend passes beneath what was once a large hall, long since ruined. In 1602-4 Lord Edzell added the north-west tower. The castle was probably never finished, and the north-east range is incomplete. It is thought that Lord Edzell became more interested in his garden than the castle.

Edzell was the seat of the Lindsays of Glenesk who acquired the lands by marriage in 1358. Previously the owners were the Stirlings, their motte visible from the present castle. A fragment of an early Christian cross found nearby is located in the Summer House. Mary, Queen of Scots visited in August 1562. Cromwell took the castle in 1651. The Lindsays retained Edzell until 1715 when David sold it to the Earl of Panmure. He was deprived of his estates for his Jacobite adherences. The castle was stripped for building materials in 1764, and one of the turrets can still be pointed out in Edzell village. Ownership passed to the Earl of Dalhousie whose descendant still retains it.

## Glamis Castle

| | |
|---|---|
| *Location* | Glamis, Forfar, Angus, DD8 1RJ. |
| | OS Map 54: NO 386480. |
| *Facilities* | ⬚ ▲ ⊞ ⚓ ✕ ♿ |
| *Owner* | Earl of Strathmore and Kinghorne. |
| *Tel* | 01307 840242/840393. |
| *Open* | Apr-Oct, Mon-Sun. |
| *Entry* | ◑ |

Glamis Castle is a particularly grand, large chateau-style castle, owned by the Lyon and Bowes-Lyon family from 1372 until the present day. It has close royal connections as Queen Elizabeth the Queen Mother is a member of the family, and her daughter Princess Margaret was born here.

Guided tours take one through sumptuously furnished rooms,

commencing with the dining room in a wing of 1798. The vaulted crypt is in the original tower, and a secret chamber is said to be located here. A minor stair leads down to the castle well. The principal, wide, turnpike dates to 1600, and leads up to the drawing room in what was the great hall. Also vaulted, it has a plaster ceiling and great fireplace.

The chapel has amazing painted panels of 1688 by Jacob de Wet. These depict the saints and Christ, with St Simon wearing glasses and Christ donning a hat! The billiard room doubles as a library and is located in the 1770s wing. The ceiling, however, is of 1903. Tapestries of 1680 hang over the bookcases. Three rooms make up the Royal Apartments. They were converted in 1923 following the marriage of Lady Elizabeth to Prince (later King) George. Duncan's Hall is where Macbeth slew Duncan, according to Shakespeare. It is a plain vault with prison off it. The Blue Room is now an exhibition room with notable family relics, including the watch left by the Old Pretender in the castle. The coach house has another exhibition on estate life past and present. Glamis has many ghostly legends.

# Edinburgh, Lothians
and Fife

# ⌂ *Aberdour Castle*

| | |
|---|---|
| *Location* | Aberdour, Fife. |
| | OS Maps 65, 66: NT 192854. |
| *Facilities* | 🏠▲⚓♿✕☕ |
| *Owner* | Historic Scotland. |
| *Tel* | 01383 860519. |
| *Open* | Apr-Sep, Mon-Sun; Oct-Mar, Sat-Thu. |
| *Entry* | ☝ |

Aberdour is an attractive castle built in three distinct stages, the most recent of which is still roofed. The original tower-house was built in the 14th century and part of a fallen corner now sits precariously below the ruins. The central range, which contained a kitchen in the vaulted ground floor and bed chambers above, was added in the 16th century. The east range was built between 1606 and 1648 by William, Earl of Morton. The ground floor contains a stable and exhibition room; the upper floor a most attractive gallery, 63ft long, with furniture and mediaeval music. A couple of small rooms are located off the gallery.

The grounds contain a 16th-century beehive doocot, with 600 nests, sundials, 50ft-deep well, gardens and walled terraces. The walled garden was for some time a bowling green.

Aberdour has been in Douglas ownership since 1342. James, 4th Earl of Morton is noted as being a Regent and murderer of Darnley, second husband of Mary, Queen of Scots. In 1642 the 7th Earl of Morton made Aberdour his principal seat, remaining as such until 1725 when the Douglas family moved to Aberdour House. The castle remained occupied successively as a barrack, school, Masonic hall and house, until 1924 when it came into state care.

# 🏰 *Balgonie Castle*

| | |
|---|---|
| *Location* | Markinch, Fife, KY7 6HQ. |
| | OS Map 59: NO 313007. |
| *Facilities* | 🛈 ♿ 🅿 |
| *Owner* | Raymond Morris. |
| *Tel* | 01592 750119. |
| *Open* | All Year, Mon-Sun. |
| *Entry* | 🅟 |

The 14th-century sandstone ashlar tower of Balgonie rises at the corner of a ruinous courtyard, with the tower restored by David Maxwell in 1975. In 1985 the castle was sold to the present owner, the artist and craftsman Raymond Morris.

The guided tour starts with the three vaults on the ground floor of the 17th-century Leslie block, home of the Covenanter, Alexander Leslie, who was created Lord Balgonie and Earl of Leven. The west vault was the kitchen, now a workshop. To the east are two linked vaults forming a chapel, now with rescued pews. The upper floors are ruins. The apartments in the main tower are reached by a wide staircase where there once was a gap and wooden bridge for defence. The vaulted ground floor has narrow slit windows. The first floor vault, the great hall, has larger windows but surprisingly no fireplace, and only two holes in the roof. It is adorned with banners, pikes and a modern minstrels gallery. The second floor has a sitting room filled with models of the castle, and examples of the present laird's collection of heraldry. The south-west gate is protected by a guard room with shot-holes and a vaulted roof. Off it is the prison.

Balgonie was originally built by Sir John Sibbald and passed to his son-in-law, Sir Robert Lundie. In the 17th century it was acquired by Alexander Leslie, whose family retained it until 1824. It was then acquired by the Balfours, but allowed to become a ruin. Rob Roy MacGregor stayed here with 200 clansmen in 1716.

## Blackness Castle

| | |
|---|---|
| *Location* | Blackness, Bo'ness, West Lothian. |
| | OS Map 65: NT 056802. |
| *Facilities* | |
| *Owner* | Historic Scotland. |
| *Tel* | 01506 834807. |
| *Open* | Apr-Sep, Mon-Sun; Oct-Mar, Sat-Thu. |
| *Entry* | |

Likened to a ship from its shape and location, Blackness has been a place of defence from when it was built in the 1440s until after World War I. Originally built by the Crichtons, it was gifted to the Crown in 1453 and used as a State Prison until 1707; as a Garrison until 1870 and then as an ammunition depot until 1912, when it was placed into care.

The castle was strengthened in the 16th century as an artillery fortress and was besieged by Cromwell in 1650. Of the many folk imprisoned here, the list includes Cardinal Beaton, Lord Ochiltree, John Welsh and Adam Blackadder, who complained that the dungeon was 'full of puddocks and toads'.

The outer courtyard at Blackness contains a barracks and officers' quarters. The castle proper has a Stern, or South Tower, Central Tower and North Tower which contains a prison and pit. The

Central Tower is a four storey block with turnpike at the corner, the lowest floor having a great boss of rock in it. Extensive views are obtained from the parapet.

The South Tower has many vaulted rooms and replica windows, the great hall having window seats, minstrel's gallery and adjoining kitchen. The courtyard wall has a parapet walk which can be airy above the crashing waves of the Firth of Forth.

## Craigmillar Castle

| Location | Craigmillar Castle Road, Edinburgh. |
| --- | --- |
| | OS Map 66: NT 288709. |
| Facilities | |
| Owner | Historic Scotland. |
| Tel | 0131 661 4445. |
| Open | Apr-Sep, Mon-Sun; Oct-Mar, Sat-Thu. |
| Entry | |

Craigmillar stands on a 300ft-hill on the southern side of Edinburgh. Built in the early-15th century by the Prestons, it was sold in 1660 to the Gilmours. The L-shaped tower is the oldest part, and a curtain wall and other ranges were added in the late-15th and -16th centuries. At either end of the outer courtyard is a chapel and church. The former dates from 1520 and contains Gilmour graves; the latter was formed in 1687 from a 16th-century block. On the south of the castle is a dry fish pond.

The inner court, which has two old pines in it, gives access to the tower and the Gilmour Apartments of 1661. A new entrance in the east range gives access via a wide turnpike to the old tower, the original entrance of which is in the re-entrant. There are a number of fireplaces dating to 1500 and a fine lord's hall, with window seats, and a buttery off it. Craigmillar was burned in 1544 but rebuilt. Mary, Queen of Scots, was a regular visitor, and it was here the plot to kill Darnley was laid. The castle was in ruins by the 18th century when the Gilmours moved to The Inch, and proposals in 1842 to restore it as the Scottish home of Queen Victoria came to nothing. It was placed in care in 1946.

## Crichton Castle

| | |
|---|---|
| *Location* | Crichton, Pathhead, Midlothian. OS Map 66: NT 380611. |
| *Facilities* | 🏛 ♿ |
| *Owner* | Historic Scotland. |
| *Tel* | 01875 320017. |
| *Open* | Apr-Sep, Mon-Sun. |
| *Entry* | ⊙ |

A track from Crichton Church leads south to Crichton Castle, which is a large and impressive structure perched above the Tyne. The oldest part, the tower on the east front, was erected by John Crichton in 1400, and was vaulted. A prison was located on the lower floor. His son, Chancellor Crichton, added a fine range to the south, and created a new entrance pend, vaulted stores, and a new hall above. The south range has some fine stonework. He also added a new block to the north and west, creating a great courtyard castle. In about 1580 Francis Stewart, 5th Earl of Bothwell, extended the castle, and added the extremely grand arcaded and diamond-faceted wall to the courtyard. He also added the fine stairway within this, to make it the first straight stair in Scotland, and he ornamented it with carved pillars and ceiling slabs. The castle has many vaulted rooms to explore, some being kitchens, bakehouses, or pantries. The kitchen in the west range has a huge double fireplace. The older kitchen adjoining has a slop-chute and open ceiling flue. The well in the loggia is deep. A postern doorway is located in the west wall. The present entrance was created in 1585, and the original was blocked off and converted to a cellar.

Externally the castle is noted for its oriel window, corbel courses, turrets, arches and large corbels. Just south of the castle is the old stable block, with its horse-shoe window a distinctive feature. The buttresses are additions, making it look like a chapel, for which it has been mistaken in the past.

Crichton was the seat of the Crichtons of that Ilk until 1483. Sir Patrick Hepburn was given the barony by James IV, along with the earldom of Bothwell. Mary, Queen of Scots attended a wedding here in 1562. The Earldom passed to the Stewarts, as did the castle, until around 1650. In 1926 the castle was placed into care by Henry Burn Callander.

## Dirleton Castle

| | |
|---|---|
| *Location* | Dirleton, East Lothian. |
| | OS Map 66: NT 515839. |
| *Facilities* | ▲□ 🏛 |
| *Owner* | National Trust for Scotland/Historic Scotland. |
| *Tel* | 01620 850330. |
| *Open* | All Year, Mon-Sun. |
| *Entry* | ☞ |

This massive ruin stands on a rock in attractive gardens which have a beehive doocot and bowling green. Built by the De Vaux family around 1225, it was sieged in 1298 by Edward I. Extended by the Halyburtons and Ruthvens, it was abandoned in 1650 following the attack by General Monk. The castle was taken into state care and gifted to the National Trust by B.C.E. Brooke in 1981.

The original entrance to the castle is located on the opposite side of the ruins from the visitor centre. A wooden bridge has replaced the drawbridge and gives access through the entry to the close. To the left is a massive 13th-century round tower. Within it are two apartments, both are hexagonal and the upper is the lord's chamber, with umbrella-vaulted roof, window seats and a large fireplace. The 16th-century Ruthven lodging is an addition, and the first floor contains a hall. The east range of the castle dates from the 14th and 15th centuries, though in some places 13th-century masonry survives. A kitchen with two huge fireplaces, a bakehouse, three vaulted cellars and a large hall over are found in the east range. The latter room has a grand buffet in the south wall. Below the dais chamber is the chapel and priest's room, with the prison and pit below them.

## ♜ *Edinburgh Castle*

| *Location* | Castle Rock, Edinburgh, EH1. |
| | OS Map 66: NT 251735. |
| *Facilities* | ⌂ ♨ ♿ ♨ ✕ ♿ |
| *Owner* | Historic Scotland. |
| *Tel* | 0131 225 9846. |
| *Open* | All year, Mon-Sun. |
| *Entry* | ◑ |

The most famous Scottish castle, Edinburgh is instantly recognisable, perched on its rock in the centre of the capital city. From the Esplanade one crosses the dry ditch and passes through the 1886 gatehouse, which has statues of Sir William Wallace and Robert Bruce. From the Lower Ward one walks through the portcullis gate, the lower half of which dates from the 16th century, the upper part (Argyle Tower) to 1886. On the right of the Middle Ward is the Argyle Battery (with the famous One o' Clock Gun) and 18th-century cart shed. Behind this are military museums in the Ordnance Store and Hospital. The Governor's House and New Barracks are still used for military purposes. Passing through Foog's Gate one enters the Upper Ward, with St Margaret's Chapel on the left, dating from the 12th century making it the oldest part of the castle. This is a very simple, but dignified building. Entry is made to Crown Square, on the east side of which is the Palace. It contains old rooms and the Honours of Scotland, or crown jewels, along with the recently-returned Stone of Scone. The south side has the 16th-century Great Hall, with the huge hammerbeam roof, built by James IV. On show are many examples of arms.

The Queen Anne Building (west side) contains a military museum. The Scottish National War Memorial on the north, dating from 1923 and designed by Robert Lorimer, contains earlier work. Within are memorials to those Scots who died in the Great War, their names recorded in books of remembrance. The Castle Vaults contain the large 15th-century cannon, Mons Meg, and the French prison a series of cells.

Edinburgh rock has been fortified for thousands of years, Bronze Age relics having been discovered in excavations. The oldest record of 'Din Eidyn' dates from around AD 600. The castle has basically been in royal and government hands ever since.

The castle has many facilities for the disabled, as well as Braille plaques.

# 🏛 *Hailes Castle*

| | |
|---|---|
| *Location* | Hailes, East Linton, East Lothian. OS Map 67: NT 574758. |
| *Facilities* | 📖 ♿ |
| *Owner* | Historic Scotland. |
| *Tel* | 0131 668 8800. |
| *Open* | All Year, Mon-Sun. |
| *Entry* | Free. |

Hailes Castle stands on a rock above the River Tyne, and its oldest parts date from the 13th century. These are the central tower, built of red sandstone, with the curtain wall to the east of this, and the stairway down to the well. The tower contains a pit prison but was altered in later years to form a doocot, the nesting boxes of which still survive. Some are carved from solid stones. The western tower was added in the late-14th century, as was the rebuilt south curtain wall. This tower has a vaulted basement and pit prison. Living quarters formerly existed above. In the 15th century a new block was added between the two towers. Its lower floor was vaulted and contained a bakehouse with oven and bread trough. The upper floor was a chapel with aumbry and piscina. A postern leads out to the riverbank. Only the foundations survive of the east range.

Hailes was probably built by the Dunbars, who were Earls of the March. The Hepburns added the west tower. In 1567 ownership passed to the Stewarts, followed by the Setons. It was destroyed in 1650 by Cromwell's troops and remained in ruins thereafter, though it was used as a granary for a time. The Earl of Balfour passed the building into state care in 1926.

# 🏰 *Kellie Castle*

| | |
|---|---|
| *Location* | Carnbee, Pittenweem, Fife, KY10 2RF. |
| | OS Map 59: NO 520052. |
| *Facilities* | 🏚️▲⛲♿♨️⛩️ |
| *Owner* | National Trust for Scotland. |
| *Tel* | 01333 720271. |
| *Open* | Easter; May-Sep, Mon-Sun; Oct, Sat-Sun. |
| *Entry* | ◖ |

A spectacular tower-house with three towers and a linking block, Kellie is well preserved and furnished. Entry is made by a lesser door in the west front. To the left is a vaulted room with video presentation. It is the base of the oldest, late-14th-century tower. The tour passes the gift-shop to the main staircase in the south-west tower of 1606. The drawing room is furnished in the Georgian style. Off it is a vault in the north-west tower, which was converted into a chapel in the 1940s by Hew Lorimer. The dining room has richly painted panels and tapestries. The Vine Room has a ceiling with plaster vines and a painted roundel by De Wet. The tour also includes the dressing room, the Earl's room, the Professor's room, a nursery on the top floor of the south-western tower, the Blue bedroom and Lorimer room below. This has changing exhibitions on the work of the architect, Sir Robert Lorimer, as well as the artist John Henry Lorimer, and the sculptor, Hew Lorimer. Examples of their work adorn the castle. The vaulted kitchen on the ground floor has a black range and numerous old utensils.

The castle, which has many turrets, chimneys, carved panels and corbie-stepped gables, was begun in the 14th century. The East tower was added in 1573 – perhaps a courtyard or low buildings were located between. In 1606 the linking block and the south-west tower were added. Originally owned by the Siward family, it passed to the Oliphants. It was sold in 1613 to the Erskines who were created Earls of Kellie in 1619. Abandoned by 1860, it was leased and ultimately purchased by Professor James Lorimer. It was bought by the Trust from the Lorimers in 1970.

## 🏰 *Lauriston Castle*

| | |
|---|---|
| *Location* | Cramond Road South, Davidson's Mains, Edinburgh, EH4 5QD. |
| | OS Map 66: NT 203761. |
| *Facilities* | ♣ ⌷ ♿ |
| *Owner* | City of Edinburgh Council. |
| *Tel* | 0131 336 2060. |
| *Open* | Apr-Oct, Sat-Thu; Nov-Mar, Sat-Sun. |
| *Entry* | ◕ |

As Lauriston exists today, it is a very fine Edwardian mansion. Purchased in 1902 by William Reid of the furniture manufacturer, Morison and Company, the building reflects his interests in furniture, Blue John ornaments, and the arts. The castle was left to the nation in trust in 1926 and the building has been kept just as it was in the Reids' time.

The original T-shaped tower, at the south-west corner, was erected in the 1590s by Archibald Napier, father of the inventor of Logarithms. It has four storeys, pepperpot turrets and spiral stairs. The rest of the mansion was added in 1827 to the plans of William

Burn, and others later. Guided tours of the fully furnished house commence at the stair hall, leading to the inner hall. The oak room has a secret apartment off it, containing the laird's lug, and two hidden safes. The library, with its pine ceiling, is a grand room, with a study in the turret and a secret doorway through the bookshelves. The drawing and sitting rooms afford fine views over the croquet lawns and the Forth to Fife. The house had modern plumbing for its time, as Mrs Reid's brother was in that trade. Other owners of Lauriston over the years include the Dalgleish's, Laws and Allans.

## Lennoxlove Castle

| *Location* | Haddington, East Lothian, EH41 4NZ. |
|---|---|
|  | OS Map 66: NT515720. |
| *Facilities* | ▯ ▲ ⚲ ⚲ ⚲ |
| *Owner* | Duke of Hamilton and Brandon. |
| *Tel* | 01620 823720/822156. |
| Open | Easter; May-Sep, Wed, Sat, Sun. |
| *Entry* | ● |

Lennoxlove was named after the Duchess of Lennox – the model for Britannia on pre-decimal coins. Previously known as Lethington Castle, it was the seat of the Maitlands. The 15th-century tower has a double-storey cap-house and corbelled parapet. The 1670s east wing was remodelled in the early 19th century. Lennoxlove passed to Lord Blantyre in the 18th century, and in 1900 to Sir David Baird. His son, William, employed Robert Lorimer to restore the building. The castle was bought by the Duke of Hamilton in 1946.

Guided tours commence in the front hall, ascending the main

stair to the China Room. A bedroom contains a unique four-poster, gifted by Princess Pauline, sister of Napoleon. The Stewart room has portraits of the monarchs; the Damask Room a table gifted by Charles II. The Yellow Sitting Room and Blue Room are, like the rest of the castle, adorned with portraits. The old tower contains relics of Mary, Queen of Scots, including her death mask, ring and casket. A side room contains bagpipes, swords and pipes. The 37ft-deep well is passed on the way to the vaulted great hall, which is a magnificent room with Flemish tapestries and large fireplace. The latter was added by the Bairds. The spiral stair descends to the lower vault, now converted to a chapel. Here also is the original yett and dungeon. A passage with funeral lozenges leads to the 20th-century room, which contains mementoes of the Dukes of Hamilton, the Nazi Rudolph Hess, the first flight over Everest, and a collection of early 20th-century motorbikes.

## Ravenscraig Castle

| Location | Off Dysart Road, Kirkcaldy, Fife. |
| | OS Map 59: NT 291925. |
| Facilities | ⊞ ㅎ |
| Owner | Historic Scotland. |
| Tel | 0131 668 8800. |
| Open | All Year, Mon-Sun. |
| Entry | Free. |

Ravenscraig Castle was built on a rocky promontory between two shingle beaches. Two mellow stone towers, with rounded fronts, face the mainland, with a footbridge crossing a dry ditch to the entrance gateway. On the west is the oldest tower. The ground floor is vaulted, and the upper floor contains a large fireplace, with various mural chambers and masons' marks. The interior stonework is blackened. The upper floors have gone, but one can see the various fireplaces and chambers. Within a little courtyard are three latrine chutes.

The east tower is lower, but has deeper foundations. At its base, within the ditch, are steps hewn from the solid rock, originally used to lead horses to a stable. The range between the towers was to have been a great hall, but it was never finished and instead was used as a gun emplacement. On the promontory are remnants of other buildings, including a kitchen, bread oven and large dough trough.

Ravenscraig was acquired by King James II in 1460 and the royal mason, Henry Merlzioun, began work. In 1470 James III swapped the castle with Lord Sinclair for the earldom of Orkney. Various other kings have visited. The Sinclairs retained possession until 1898. In 1955 it was taken into state care.

## St Andrews Castle

| | |
|---|---|
| *Location* | The Scores, St Andrews, Fife. |
| | OS Map 59: NO 513169. |
| *Facilities* | |
| *Owner* | Historic Scotland. |
| *Tel* | 01334 477196. |
| *Open* | All Year, Mon-Sun. |
| *Entry* | |

St Andrews Castle is less well known than the cathedral, but it is every bit as interesting. From the visitor centre one can enter either by a lesser gateway, or else over the bridge and through the Renaissance gateway of 1555-8. In vaults to either side are the false starts to a counter mine of 1546-7, which is perhaps the most notable feature of the ruins. It is possible to see in the stonework where the outer wall was strengthened in 1539-71. The courtyard contains a well. The north-east tower has two vaults on the ground floor, the base of a bread oven and a water gate. The sea tower contains a bottle dungeon 24ft-deep, located in a vault. The gate tower has traces of an older gateway (which had a drawbridge) of Bishop Walter Traill, 1385-1401. The east range was mostly destroyed by sea erosion, and collapsed in 1801.

The mine and counter-mine of 1546-7 is one of the most unique features of the castle. The Earl of Arran's men were digging a tunnel into the castle and those within dug outwards to try and stop them. They could only go by sounds passing through the rocks, and thus made a few false starts. Nevertheless the two tunnels did meet. Blocked up for many years, they were only rediscovered in 1879 and today visitors can make their way along the passages.

A stronghold of the bishops of St Andrews Cathedral, the castle passed to the Crown in 1587. By the late-17th century it was in ruins, and the stone was used to rebuild the harbour.

# Scotstarvit Tower

| Location | Scotstarvit, Craigrothie, Cupar, Fife. OS Map 59: NO 370112. |
|---|---|
| Facilities | 📖 |
| Owner | National Trust for Scotland/Historic Scotland. |
| Tel | 01334 653127. |
| Open | Easter; May-Sep, Mon-Sun; Oct, Sat-Sun. |
| Entry | Free. Obtain key at Hill of Tarvit house (NTS). |

Scotstarvit is a very fine and complete ashlar tower built on a rock outcrop. L-shaped in plan, the arched doorway leads to the vaulted ground floor, and the corbels survive for the missing wooden entresol floor. The turnpike stair in the wing leads to the first floor hall with its large fireplace, windows with seats, slop-chute and laird's lug. The ceiling is of timber. There are some carved stones on the floor here, one of 1723. The second floor is again vaulted, the third having a missing timber ceiling. There may have been a doocot in this storey, there being two block openings for birds in the walls. A fireplace which existed here is now incorporated in the Hill of Tarvit. The stair, which is 75 steps high, is followed up to the cap-house, with stone roof. Over the doorway is a panel with the initials SIS DAD IS AD 1627. The parapet walk can be followed right round the tower, and the roof is of flagstones.

Tarvit tower was erected between 1550-79 for the Inglis's, but was purchased in 1611 by John Scot who renamed it Scotstarvit. It is his initials and those of his wife, Anne Drummond, which appear on the panel over the cap-house door. He was noted as the author of *The Staggering State of the Scots Statesmen*. The estate later passed to the Wemyss family followed by Frederick Sharp in 1904. The castle was placed in care in 1941, and gifted to the National Trust for Scotland in 1949 by Miss E C Sharp.

## Tantallon Castle

| | |
|---|---|
| *Location* | Tantallon, North Berwick, East Lothian. OS Map 67: NT 596850. |
| *Facilities* | ▢ ⛟ ♿ ⚲ |
| *Owner* | Historic Scotland. |
| *Tel* | 01620 892727. |
| *Open* | Apr-Sep, Mon-Sun; Oct-Mar, Sat-Thu. |
| *Entry* | ☉ |

Spectacularly located on its cliff-top, Tantallon shows a massive sandstone wall to the landward. Outwith this are earthworks, a doocot and an outer gate. A bridge across the ditch enters the Mid Tower, formerly the home of the keeper. Great walls extend to either side of this, and within them stairways lead to the high battlements. A further stair in the Mid Tower leads to the airy turret which has views of the castle and across the Forth to the Bass Rock. The East Tower is partially ruinous. Formerly it was five storeys in height, but one room is still roofed and has a replica gun in place. The western tower was the laird's residence, and is known as the Douglas Tower. Formerly six storeys tall, only the lower floors are now hale – the vaulted prison and garderobe. The two terminal towers have been ruinous since the attack by Cromwell in 1651. Within the courtyard is a 100ft-deep well, an incomplete sea gate, and the west wing with brew house, and a kitchen with its oven. Over the vaults is the hall, with the profile of the roof timbers surviving in stone.

Tantallon was built by the 'Red' Douglases in the 14th century. It was attacked in 1528 by King James V but was rebuilt. Queen Victoria visited in 1878. It was taken into state care in 1924.

# Glasgow, Lanarkshire and the West of Scotland

# 🏠 *Bothwell Castle*

| | |
|---|---|
| *Location* | Uddingston, Lanarkshire. |
| | OS Map 64: NS 688593. |
| *Facilities* | 🅿 ♨ ♿ 🚻 |
| *Owner* | Historic Scotland. |
| *Tel* | 01698 816894. |
| *Open* | Apr-Sep, Mon-Sun; Oct-Mar, Sat-Thu. |
| *Entry* | 🅟 |

Built of red sandstone on a rock outcrop in a bend of the Clyde, Bothwell is one of the most important early castles in Scotland. There remains part of the great 13th-century round tower, formerly having four floors, and decorated with ornate stonework. This tower was partially demolished in 1337, but a straight wall was built across one side bringing it back into use. The inner courtyard lies beyond the ditch, and at the east end was a great hall with traceried windows over three vaults. The hall had a large dais window and minstrel's gallery. Remains of the earlier hall can be seen below in the turnpike and service stairs, and the former fireplaces. The chapel was at first floor level, with the piscina, Holy Water stoup and sacrament house still surviving. The castle sports a former portcullis and drawbridge mechanism. Some stone shot and cannonballs, along with various carved stones found during excavations, are to be found in one of the vaults.

Bothwell was built by the Morays, and passed to Douglas ownership in 1362. It was forfeited to the Crown in 1445. The castle was acquired by the Douglas Earl of Forfar in 1669 and used as a quarry for his new house. It was passed into state care by the Earls of Home in 1935.

# 🏰 *Brodick Castle*

| | |
|---|---|
| *Location* | Brodick, Island of Arran, KA27 8HY. OS Map 69: NS 015379. |
| *Facilities* | ⛺🅿🍴♿🚻✕🏛 |
| *Owner* | National Trust for Scotland. |
| *Tel* | 01770 302202. |
| *Open* | Apr-Oct, Mon-Sun. |
| *Entry* | ◖ |

The oldest part of the castle dates from the 13th century but was added to in the 14th century, and later in 1558 (the East Tower), 1652, and in 1844 (the West Tower), the latter designed by the architect James Gillespie Graham.

From the entrance hall, with 87 stags heads, one reaches the Duchess's dressing room, bedroom and boudoir, all sumptuously furnished. The boudoir landing, with large paintings, has an arcade to the stair. The gallery leads along the length of the building. Off it are the drawing room, with its heraldic ceiling, the Old Library and the dining room, with their wood panelling and ornate ceilings. The China room has many examples of porcelain, and a stair descends to the kitchen and scullery. These contain various utensils from the past, including brass, pewter, and an unusual spit turner. Bruce's room, which is vaulted and was once used as a prison, is reached by a small staircase. There are many horse-racing mementos in the castle, as well as silver, porcelain and artwork from the Hamilton, Beckford and Rochford collections.

Brodick was built by the Crown, but the castle passed to the Hamiltons in 1503. They remained owners, as Earls of Arran and

Dukes of Hamilton, until the death of Mary, Duchess of Montrose, heiress of the 12th Duke of Hamilton. The National Trust for Scotland took the castle over in 1958. The 6,603-acre Goatfell estate is also owned by the Trust.

## Craignethan Castle

| | |
|---|---|
| *Location* | Tillietudlem, Crossford, Lanark. OS Map 72: NS 816464. |
| *Facilities* | 🏛 🚻 ♿ 🅿 ☕ |
| *Owner* | Historic Scotland. |
| *Tel* | 01555 860364. |
| *Open* | Apr-Sep, Mon-Sun; Mar, Oct, Sat-Sun. |
| *Entry* | 🅖 |

Perched on a promontory between the River Nethan and a minor burn, Craignethan Castle is a fascinating yellow sandstone fortress, perhaps the last private castle of its type in Scotland. Built between 1530-45 by Sir James Hamilton, the whole structure exhibits many unique features. From the approach avenue one passes through the outer gate into the outer court. To the left is a doocot tower of around 1579, to the right the Scots domestic range known as Andrew Hay's House, erected in 1665. A footbridge crosses the ditch to the inner court or close, where the great west rampart is now little more than foundations. A spiral stair drops down into the caponier, which is a unique defensive structure that allows those defending the castle to shoot at anyone crossing the ditch. The caponier was only discovered in 1962.

The tower is entered from the close. A stair to the right drops into cellars – one, perhaps, was a prison. The hall takes up the ground floor, as does the kitchen, though only a serving hatch connects them. Only part of the hall's vault survives, but the minstrel's gallery remains. Above are remnants of four chambers and a mezzanine floor. To the east of the tower are vaulted cellars, one was a brewhouse, with others used as a kitchen and stores. The roofed kitchen tower may have had a first floor chapel.

Craignethan remained in Hamilton hands (for a time Earls of Arran) until 1659 when it was acquired by Andrew Hay. The tower was probably ruinous, hence the new house erected by him. It is claimed that Craignethan was the inspiration for 'Tillietudlem Castle' in Sir Walter Scott's *Old Mortality*. Mary, Queen of Scots visited a couple of times.

# 🏠 Crookston Castle

| | |
|---|---|
| *Location* | Towerside Crescent, Pollok, Glasgow. |
| | OS Map 64: NS 526627. |
| *Facilities* | ♿ |
| *Owner* | National Trust for Scotland/Historic Scotland. |
| *Tel* | 0141 226 4826. |
| *Open* | All year, Mon-Sun. |
| *Entry* | Free. |

The 15th-century castle stands on a mound in the midst of a housing estate. The knoll has a moat around its top, enclosing a flat courtyard in which stands the castle tower. The main hall has a parallelogram plan, with square towers at the corners, two of which are gone. The third is one storey tall, the fourth rises to five floors, and the uppermost was rebuilt in 1847. A series of ladders lead to the viewing platform, affording panoramas over Glasgow.

The entrance doorway is adjacent to the north-east tower, leading to the vaulted ground floor. A lesser stair in the main tower leads to a guardroom, below which is the dungeon. A stair in the north wall climbs to the main hall, which originally had a vaulted ceiling 28ft high. A spiral stair leads up to the second floor of the tower.

Crookston was built in the 12th century by Robert de Croc but in 1330 was bought by Sir Alan Stewart. In 1361 it was granted to his descendant Stewart of Darnley. Henry, Lord Darnley, was noted as the wife of Mary, Queen of Scots; both visited in 1565. In 1757 the castle was bought by the Maxwells of Pollok, who, by gifting it to the National Trust in 1931, made it the Trust's first property.

## Culzean Castle

| | |
|---|---|
| *Location* | Maybole, Ayrshire, KA19 8LE. |
| | OS Map 70: NS 233102. |
| *Facilities* | ⊞▲⚑♿✕♨ |
| *Owner* | National Trust for Scotland. |
| *Tel* | 01655 760269. |
| *Open* | Apr-Oct, Mon-Sun. |
| *Entry* | ◗ |

Set in 568 acres of policies, Culzean is a magnificent Robert Adam castle of 1772-92, built for the Earl of Cassillis. Situated on a cliff top, an older Kennedy tower house was incorporated at the time of building. The entrance door leads into the armoury, the walls of which are covered with swords and guns. The tour passes through the

Old Eating Room, dining room, dramatic oval staircase and grand circular saloon, which overlooks the Firth of Clyde with magnificent views to Arran and Kintyre. The anteroom is followed by Lord Cassillis' Bedroom, First Drawing Room, Picture Room, and State Bedroom, each magnificently furnished. There is a very fine selection of Adam ceilings and furnishings, portraits and paintings, including ceiling paintings. A special presentation details the life of General Eisenhower and there are a number of model ships, with even a boat-shaped cradle, reflecting the family's shipbuilding connections.

The policies contain many walks, and other notable buildings, such as the Home Farm, which is now a visitor centre.

Culzean has been the home of the Kennedy family since the 14th century. In 1945 the 5th Marquis of Ailsa gifted the castle and estate to the Trust, and it quickly became its most popular property.

## Dean Castle

| | |
|---|---|
| *Location* | Dean Road, Kilmarnock, Ayrshire. OS Map 70: NS 437394. |
| *Facilities* | ⌂ ▲ ⚑ ⚐ ♿ |
| *Owner* | East Ayrshire Council. |
| *Tel* | 01563 522702/574916. |
| *Open* | All Year, Mon-Sun. |
| *Entry* | ☺ |

Located in a 200-acre country park, the keep of Dean Castle dates from c.1350, with a palace and barmkin added in 1460. A Victorian mansion is now the castle shop, where guided tours commence. The castle was burned in 1735 and lay in ruins until the restoration of

1908-46. The gatehouse was added in 1936.

The ground floor of the keep is vaulted. The tour ascends the modern stair to the great hall, which is furnished with arms and tapestries. There is a minstrels' gallery at one end. Off the guard room is a pit. The second floor is the solar, formerly two rooms, with wooden ceiling and chapel in the window bay. A collection of old musical instruments is on display. The turnpike leads up to the open battlements which are reached through a caphouse.

The palace has a vaulted kitchen on the ground floor, with old utensils, and oven in the ingle. The dining room above has a plaster ceiling, brought from Balcomie Castle. Heraldic banners commemorate former owners. A stair leads to a chamber, with panelled walls and a plaster ceiling.

Dean Castle was owned by the Boyd family until 1748. In 1786 the Scotts (later Scott-Ellis) bought it, with the 9th Lord Howard de Walden giving the castle to Kilmarnock in 1975.

 ## *Dumbarton Castle*

| Location | Castle Road, Dumbarton. |
| --- | --- |
| | OS Map 64: NS 400745. |
| Facilities | |
| Owner | Historic Scotland. |
| Tel | 01389 732167. |
| Open | Apr-Sep, Mon-Sun; Oct-Mar, Sat-Thu. |
| Entry | |

Dumbarton Castle has the longest recorded history of any fort in Britain. Built on a volcanic plug, this was the ancient capital of

Strathclyde, which was an independent kingdom until 1018. Mary, Queen of Scots left from here for France in 1548 at the age of five. The rock has been defended until modern times, and was last used in World War II.

The rock is split in two, with a level area between which was the site of the ancient buildings. Today only the French Prison is there, plus the well. This is reached from the King George Battery and Governor's House (both of 1735), passing through the guardhouse (16th century) and the 14th-century portcullis arch, which is the oldest surviving structure. The guardhouse has a display room, with mediaeval grave slabs and more modern uniforms. From Castle Road 344 steps climb up to the White Tower, with the highest point at 240ft, with a viewpoint, flagstaff and remnants of a tower. The east rock, or The Beak, has a magazine dated to 1748. It was designed by William Skinner to store 150 barrels of gunpowder.

The whole rock is of interest for its fortifications, seven batteries with 19th-century guns, steep paths, and spectacular views of Ben Lomond and the Firth of Clyde.

# Dundonald Castle

| | |
|---|---|
| *Location* | Dundonald, Ayrshire. |
| | OS Map 70: NS 363345. |
| *Facilities* | |
| *Owner* | Historic Scotland. |
| *Tel* | 01563 850201. |
| *Open* | Apr-Sep, Mon-Sun. |
| *Entry* | |

A massive pile crowning a prominent hill, Dundonald Castle can be seen for many miles around. The present ruins date from the third castle to occupy the site, and before that there was a fort of the Dark Ages. The first castle was erected in the late-12th century, made mainly of wood. The next castle was erected in the late-13th century by Alexander Stewart, but it was destroyed in the Wars of Independence. The well from this building survives outwith the present castle, and part of a round tower is incorporated in the north-west corner.

The present castle was erected around 1371, when Robert II was crowned. The castle is three storeys high. The lower vault formerly had a wooden floor. The modern platform there now occupies the approximate original level; the ground floor was used for storage. The upper floor was the laigh hall, with its great barrel-vault a distinctive feature. A tight spiral stair in the south-east corner leads up to the second floor, where the great hall once was. It is now roofless. However, its grandness is still apparent, as the missing vault has stone ribs and ornate arches adorn the walls.

The bedrooms must have been located in the southern extension which was added c. 1450. Here also was the ground floor prison, with fireplace, and a dark pit below. The Stewarts owned Dundonald from around 1150 until 1482 when it was sold to the Cathcarts. In 1526 it passed to the Wallaces, but by 1650 it was in ruins, the family having moved to Old Auchans nearby. Tradition states that some stone was taken from the castle to build the new house. James Boswell and Samuel Johnson visited the ruins in 1773. The Cochrane family, the chief of which has the title Earl of Dundonald, acquired the ruins later.

## Kelburn Castle

| | |
|---|---|
| *Location* | Fairlie, Largs, Ayrshire, KA29 0BE. |
| | OS Map 63: NS 217567. |
| *Facilities* | ♠♜♿♨♬ |
| *Owner* | Earl of Glasgow. |
| *Tel* | 01475 568685. |
| *Open* | Jul-Aug, Mon-Sun. |
| *Entry* | ◗ |

The Boyle family have owned Kelburn since 1140, becoming Earls of Glasgow in 1703. The first Earl assisted in the Union of Parliaments. The 7th Earl was Governor of New Zealand from 1892-7.

The Z-plan tower house was erected in 1581 by John Boyle, with the main block four storeys tall with circular towers and turrets. In 1700 the William and Mary wing was erected two storeys tall. Its mason, Robert Caldwell, built it to Lord Boyle's plans. The Victorian wing was added in 1879. The tour, bookable at the park centre, is often led by the Countess of Glasgow. It begins in the entrance hall (the wing dates from 1700), climbs the main stair (which is decorated with stags heads and crocodile-like ghariol from Africa) to the drawing room, and on to the Bastille Room in the old tower, the Victorian dining room and various bedrooms. The dining room has a view through large windows over the Plaisance to Great Cumbrae island. There are many old paintings, books, crockery, plasterwork and William Morris wallpaper.

The country park has various attractions including a museum, walks, a playground, animals, a Robert Adam memorial (1775), waterfalls and interesting trees and shrubs.

## 🏠 *Loch Doon Castle*

| | |
|---|---|
| *Location* | Craigmalloch, Loch Doon, Dalmellington, Ayrshire. OS Map 77: NX 484950. |
| *Facilities* | &#9855; |
| *Owner* | Historic Scotland. |
| *Tel* | 0131 668 8800. |
| *Open* | All Year, Mon-Sun. |
| *Entry* | Free. |

The castle takes the form of an irregular polygon, having eleven sides. This came about as it was built to fit the shape of the island, on which it formerly stood, within the loch. In 1935, when the water level was being raised for hydro-electric purposes, the castle was rebuilt in its present location, at a cost of £4,000.

Dating from the late-13th century, the castle was built by the

Earls of Carrick. In 1306 the building was taken by the English and Sir Christopher Seton, brother-in-law of the Bruce, was captured. It withstood a seige in 1335. In 1510 William Craufurd of Leifnoreis captured the castle. Around 1530 the castle was burned at the command of James V, as part of his plan to subdue the nobility of Galloway.

On entering the portcullis arch the courtyard is reached. The gateway is lower in height than the court level, as the waters of the loch originally entered the castle to allow access by boat. There is a small postern in the east wall. A large fireplace is located on the west wall. Remains of a spiral staircase are located near the centre – the later square tower which stood here was not transferred from the islet. It was probably erected after the burning.

## Lochranza Castle

| | |
|---|---|
| *Location* | Lochranza, Isle of Arran. |
| | OS Maps 62, 69: NR 933507. |
| *Facilities* | |
| *Owner* | Historic Scotland. |
| *Tel* | 0131 668 8800. |
| *Open* | Apr-Sep, Mon-Sun. |
| *Entry* | Free. |

Picturesquely located on a narrow spit of land that projects into Loch Ranza, this castle was built of grey stone with red sandstone dressings. The doorway was added in the 16th century, with the earlier doorways being blocked, one of which was located at first floor level. Over the present entrance is an empty armorial panel and a fine machiolation, from where castle defenders could drop things onto the attackers. The iron yett leads into the ground floor, with three vaulted rooms. One is a dungeon, the others were for storage. The former first floor contained a hall, later divided by a wall. A garderobe off it is located in the original stairwell. The turnpike also gives access to the kitchen, which has a service window. The south-east tower was added at a later date and is five storeys tall.

Lochranza as it is today was built by the Montgomerie family in the 16th century, but they added to an old hall house which had been built by the Menteiths in the late-13th century. The Montgomeries acquired the castle in 1452, but they lost it to the Hamiltons in 1705. In 1897 the north-east corner collapsed, being eroded by the sea, but the building had been roofless since before 1772.

## 🏠 *Newark Castle*

| | |
|---|---|
| *Location* | Castle Road, Port Glasgow, Renfrewshire. OS Map 63: NS 327745. |
| *Facilities* | 📖 ♿ ☕ |
| *Owner* | Historic Scotland. |
| *Tel* | 01475 741858. |
| *Open* | Apr-Sep, Mon-Sun. |
| *Entry* | ☛ |

Newark is a most attractive tower house built on the shores of the Clyde but now with a shipyard to one side. Other yards were located to the east, but this land is now a park. There is a doocot on the Clyde side of the tower.

The oldest parts are the tower and gateway of the 15th century.

The connecting range was added in 1597-9 by Patrick Maxwell, whose monogram is over the door. The motto THE BLISSINGIS OF GOD BE HERIN is also here, but Patrick was a wife-beater and murderer! Dressed sandstone mouldings surround the windows, and the north front is symmetrical. The castle has a fine selection of rooms to explore, the ground floor having six vaults which are open, including bakehouse, kitchen and wine cellar. A wide scale and platt stair leads to the first floor, where the great hall, with grand fireplace, is furnished with replica items. On the floor above is a long gallery with a display of old prints of Port Glasgow and a bust of John Wood, shipbuilder (1788-1860).

Newark's old tower was built by George Maxwell around 1484 and James IV visited in 1495. In 1668 George Maxwell sold ground to allow the erection of Port Glasgow. The castle was sold in 1694 and subsequently leased to tenants.

# Inverness, the Highlands and Islands

# ⌂ *Armadale Castle*

| | |
|---|---|
| *Location* | Ardvasar, Sleat, Island of Skye, IV45 8RS. |
| | OS Map 32: NG 640047. |
| *Facilities* | ♨♣♿⚓✕ |
| *Owner* | Clan Donald Lands Trust. |
| *Tel* | 01471 844227/305. |
| *Open* | Apr-Oct, Mon-Sun. |
| *Entry* | ◔ |

The 20,000-acre Armadale estate was purchased by the Clan Donald Lands Trust in 1972. The castle had been abandoned by Lord Macdonald, and much of it had to be demolished. However, the ruins of the entrance doorway and stairs of the 1815 Gillespie Graham block survive. Adjoining are the complete walls of the 1855 David Bryce block, which await restoration. Next to this is the 1790 block, totally restored and home of the Museum of the Isles, which tells the story of the Lords of the Isles and Hebridean history. This is the oldest part of the castle.

Within the grounds are the restored 1822 Gillespie Graham stables, with a restaurant, shop and holiday suite inside, and the Gardener's Cottage of 1870 which houses an exhibition area and family history library. There are gardens and woodland walks.

Armadale has only been the seat of the Macdonalds since 1790, but the land had been theirs from the 15th century, the ruins of their Caisteal Chamuis being three miles further along the coast. In 1925 the castle was abandoned in favour of the smaller Kinloch Lodge some miles to the north.

## Castle of Old Wick

| Location | Old Wick, Wick, Caithness. |
| --- | --- |
| | OS Map 12: ND 369488. |
| Facilities | None. |
| Owner | Historic Scotland. |
| Tel | 0131 668 8800. |
| Open | All Year, Mon-Sun. |
| Entry | Free. |

From the South Head of Wick Bay a footpath along the cliff top leads to the castle, passing an army shooting range. The castle stands on a narrow neck of rock between sheer cliffs. A ditch is crossed and the castle is entered on the north side of the tower. This building is little more than three stone walls, rising to three storeys, but with no floors or vaults. Remains of small windows survive, and it is possible to make out the holes where the floor joists once were. Over the ground floor window is a lintel with early graffiti – J. LEVICK HERIOTS HOSPITAL 1874. The headland beyond has grass-covered foundations of other buildings.

The castle is probably Norse in origin, perhaps built by Harald Maddadson, Earl of Caithness, in the 12th century. He was half-Orcadian, half-Scottish, his father being Earl of Atholl. The castle was held by Sir Reginald de Cheyne in the 14th century. It later passed to the Earl of Sutherland, followed by the Oliphants. In 1569 the castle was taken by the Master of Caithness, and purchased by the Earl of Caithness in 1606. It was later owned by the Dunbars, and seems perhaps to have been complete in the 1630s. The castle was for a time known as Castle Oliphant, and seamen refer to it as the Old Man of Wick.

# 🏰 *Castle Stuart*

| | |
|---|---|
| *Location* | Petty, Inverness, IV1 2JH. OS Map 27: NH 741498. |
| *Facilities* | 🎁 ♿ |
| *Owner* | Charles Stuart. |
| *Tel* | 01463 790745. |
| *Open* | May-Oct, Mon-Sun. |
| *Entry* | ◑ |

Castle Stuart is an impressive structure with a main block and towers at the southern corners. The north front is distinguished by two angled square turrets, built up on corbels. The castle was erected between 1621-5 by James Stuart, 3rd Earl of Moray. It was rebuilt to plans of James Maitland Wardrop in 1869 when the stair-cap, with open crown, was built on the west tower. The building gradually became ruinous and the roof of the central block collapsed. In 1978 Mr and Mrs Stuart, Canadian Scots, leased the building from Lord Moray and began restoration, a task which took 14 years to complete. It is now available for accommodation, with eight bedrooms.

Guided tours take one through most of the main rooms, including the Jacobean dining room, great hall with laird's lug, library and billiard room (reached by a secret doorway), oak-panelled drawing room, and whichever of the bedrooms are vacant. The top room in the east tower is said to be haunted. The battlements can also be visited, and afford views of Inverness Firth and Culloden Moor. Bonnie Prince Charlie is said to have visited the castle before Culloden, and a series of modern paintings in the great hall by W.T.J. Burton tell the story of his life. Much of the panelling is modern.

# 🏰 *Cawdor Castle*

| | |
|---|---|
| *Location* | Cawdor, Nairn, IV12 5RD. |
| | OS Map 27: NH 848498. |
| *Facilities* | ▢ ▲ ⛺ ♨ ✕ ⓹ |
| *Owner* | Earl of Cawdor. |
| *Tel* | 01667 404615. |
| *Open* | May-Oct, Mon-Sun. |
| *Entry* | ◗ |

Cawdor is a very fine castle with an ancient keep c.1380 at its core, and is surrounded by lesser wings and three courtyards. The vaulted ground floor of the tower still has the remains of a holly tree which grew on the site, and tradition says this is where the builder's donkey lay down to rest, thus choosing the tower's location. The keep rises to four main storeys, with crenellated parapet and corner turrets.

Entry to the castle is made across a drawbridge. The drawing room (great hall) has a minstrel's gallery and many family portraits. The Tapestry Room has fine Flemish tapestries dated 1682. They depict Noah and his family. The Yellow, Woodcock and Pink rooms follow, all sumptuously furnished. The Tartan Passage contains old needlework and a model of the sailing ship Victory. Off the vaulted Thorn Room is the old dungeon which, when it was discovered in 1979, contained nine tons of rubble. The yett came from Lochindorb Castle. The front stair leads to the dining room and its heraldic fireplace of 1510. When the stone for this was being brought across the drawbridge it collapsed, injuring 24 men. In this room is preserved a bronze bell of the 9th century, found at Barevan church. A modern kitchen of 1971 is followed by the original vaulted kitchen, complete with large well and copper utensils. The former larder has an unusual tricycle, fire engine and other relics, many of them from the Victorian period.

In the courtyard is a well-stocked bookshop. To the south of the castle are the flower and wild gardens, and to the north the old walled garden, with a modern maze.

The lands of 'Calder' were held by the Calders, Thanes of that Ilk, until 1510 when they passed by marriage of the then heiress, Muriel, to Sir John Campbell. The Campbells still own the estate, and were created Earls of Cawdor in 1827.

## 🏰 *Dunrobin Castle*

| | |
|---|---|
| *Location* | Golspie, Sutherland, KW10 6RR. |
| | OS Map 17: NG 247491. |
| *Facilities* | ⌂▲🏕⛲✕🛶 |
| *Owner* | Countess of Sutherland. |
| *Tel* | 01408 633177/633268. |
| *Open* | Apr-Oct, Mon-Sun. |
| *Entry* | 🍽 |

Dunrobin is a huge chateau-like castle perched on a rock, below which are extensive and attractive gardens. Its tall 'candle-snuffer' turret roofs are a distinctive feature. Built in stages, the oldest part is the central tower of the 14th century. The south-west block was added in 1641, the south block in 1785. In 1845 the whole castle was remodelled and extended to the plans of Sir Charles Barry, architect of the Houses of Parliament. Following a fire in 1915, when the castle acted as a naval hospital, Sir Robert Lorimer carried out restoration work, and created the present building. From the porte-cochere the entrance hall, covered in the arms of the Sutherland family, is reached. A stair with hunting trophies leads to the panelled dining room, former billiard room (with displays of uniforms), breakfast and drawing rooms. The latter is a very fine apartment, adorned with tapestries and affords views of the garden. The library contains ten thousand volumes and is panelled with stained sycamore. The Ladies Sitting Room, Green and Gold Room follow, and like all the apartments are finely furnished. From the passage there is a view of the original sandstone castle with its round stair tower. A suite of nursery rooms follow, and the Clan Sutherland room. Stairs round an old lift descend to the sub-hall which is full of artefacts, including a fire engine, vacuum cleaners, telephones, and ammunition, etc.

Next to the garden is a museum containing hunting trophies, taxidermy, fossils, medals, archaeological finds and an important collection of Pictish symbol stones.

Dunrobin has been owned by the Sutherland family since the 1200s, with the first Earl of Sutherland dying around 1248. The husband of the 19th Countess was created Duke of Sutherland, but on the death of the 5th Duke the castle was inherited by his niece, the present countess.

# Dunvegan Castle

| Location | Dunvegan, Island of Skye, IV55 8WF. |
| | OS Map 23: NG 247491. |
| Facilities | □ ♠ ♨ ⚓ ✕ ♿ |
| Owner | John MacLeod of MacLeod. |
| Tel | 01470 521206. |
| Open | Mar-Oct, Mon-Sun. |
| Entry | ◖ |

Built on a rock headland projecting into Loch Dunvegan, this castle has a Gothic appearance. It disguises a much older building, however, and parts of it date back to the 13th century. The wall round the courtyard (which has a well and steps down to the sea-gate) dates from this time. The keep was erected in the 14th century, the Fairy Tower around 1500. Later additions date from the 17th, 18th and 19th century. The present appearance is due to the alterations made by Robert Brown for the 25th chief, Norman MacLeod, between 1840 and 1850.

The present entrance from the crenellated courtyard leads up a stair to the first floor. The Fairy Tower has a study at this level, which was originally a bedroom within earshot of the stream. On show is a letter from Dr Samuel Johnson expressing thanks for the hospitality he received on his visit in 1773. The dining room is adorned with family portraits and furniture, with the library connected to it. Here are many old volumes, including the MacLeod Armorial, a book of arms dating from the 1580s. The drawing room in the keep was restyled in 1795. The Fairy Flag hangs there – it is an ancient clan relic which was believed to bring success in battle. Adjoining is a small tower with the prison over the dungeon, which is 13ft-deep. The lower four feet were hewn from solid rock. The Green Room contains relics of Bonnie Prince Charlie, Flora MacDonald, Rory Mor's horn, and the Dunvegan Cup – a 16th-century drinking vessel given by the O'Neills to Rory Mor. In the vaults below are ancient stones, the great sword of Dunvegan, and an exhibition on the islands of St Kilda, which belonged to the MacLeods for at least four centuries until the 1930s.

Dunvegan has been in MacLeod ownership for centuries, and the present owner is the 29th chief and a noted singer. The gardens are attractively laid out around the burn, and boat trips are available in Loch Dunvegan.

## Eilean Donan Castle

| | |
|---|---|
| *Location* | Dornie, by Kyle of Lochalsh, Ross-shire, IV40 8DX. OS Map 33: NG 881258. |
| *Facilities* | |
| *Owner* | Conchra Charitable Trust (John MacRae). |
| *Tel* | 01599 555202. |
| *Open* | Apr-Oct, Mon-Sun. |
| *Entry* | |

A causeway bridge leads to the tidal Eilean Donan on which stands this famous castle. From 1719 until 1912 the building was a ruin, but in that year, and over a twenty year period, the castle was rebuilt at a cost of a quarter of a million pounds. The plan of the complete castle was seen in a vision by Farquhar MacRae, later confirmed when original plans were discovered in Edinburgh Castle. The restorer was Lt.-Col. John MacRae-Gilstrap, whose initials and the date 1928 appear over the entrance portcullis.

The castle was originally built in 1220, and was owned by the MacKenzies of Kintail, but from 1509 the MacRaes acted as Constables of the castle on their behalf. The castle was successfully held against the Lord of the Isles in 1539. In 1719 it was garrisoned by Spanish Jacobites, but was blown up by three English frigates and left in ruins.

Entry is made through the portcullis to the courtyard. Steps lead to the main tower, and into the vaulted Billeting Room, which contains furniture, paintings, and relics. The walls are 14ft thick. The Banqueting Hall over has a wooden ceiling, a large heraldic fireplace, and collections of arms and paintings. There is a fragment of tartan which belonged to Bonnie Prince Charlie, one of his letters, a lock of hair from James III, a sword of John MacRae, the Raasay Punch Bowl from which Dr Johnson drank, and other curios. The hall has a small minstrels', or piper's, gallery, piscina and aumbry, plus the original yett, found in the 32ft-deep well in 1883. The floor above has furnished bedrooms and sitting rooms. A door is carved with the names of the Constables of Eilean Donan over the centuries. In the lower tower is a vaulted gift shop. On the north side of the castle is a MacRae war memorial to World War I.

# 🏚 *Strome Castle*

| | |
|---|---|
| *Location* | Stromemore, Lochcarron, Ross & Cromarty. |
| | OS Map 24: NG 862354. |
| *Facilities* | None. |
| *Owner* | National Trust for Scotland. |
| *Open* | All Year, Mon-Sun. |
| *Entry* | Free. |

Located at Stromemore, four miles south of Lochcarron village, Strome Castle is today a fragmentary ruin. Built on a low headland projecting into Loch Carron, the castle dates from at least the mid-15th century, for in 1472 Alan MacDonald Dubh, 12th chief of the Camerons, was appointed Constable of Strome by the Lord of Lochalsh. It passed through the female line to the MacDonalds of Glengarry.

In 1602 the castle was destroyed by Colin MacKenzie of Kintail following its seizure from the MacDonalds. This siege was undertaken by English soldiers, with the MacDonalds managing to hold out for some time. The ruins were never rebuilt.

Strome comprises of a ruinous square tower to the east with a courtyard to the west. This is entered through a gateway on the north wall. A second gateway in the west wall still leads to the headland.

Strome was presented to the Trust in 1939 by Mr C.W. Murray of Couldoran.

# Urquhart Castle

| | |
|---|---|
| *Location* | Strone, Drumnadrochit, Inverness-shire. |
| | OS Maps 26, 35: NH 531286. |
| *Facilities* | |
| *Owner* | Historic Scotland. |
| *Tel* | 01456 450551. |
| *Open* | All Year, Mon-Sun. |
| *Entry* | |

Romantically situated on Strone Point by the side of Loch Ness, Urquhart Castle is one of the better known Scottish castles. It has a complicated layout, having been developed over many centuries. From the drawbridge one enters a large irregular courtyard. To the south is the upper bailey, with various structures, including what is though to have been a smithy and the base of a round doocot. The northern half of the castle has more buildings, and here rises the tower-house at the tip of Strone Point. It has five storeys, though some floors have gone, reached by a turnpike stair. The great hall was located over the kitchen in a separate block, rising above a cliff. In the middle of the nether bailey, on a low mound, stood what was probably the chapel.

The first castle was built for Alan Durward, son-in-law of Alexander II, in the 13th century. In 1275 ownership passed to John Comyn but it was captured by the English in 1296. It passed to and fro for a number of years until in 1308 Robert the Bruce gave it to his nephew, Sir Thomas Randolph. It returned to Crown hands in 1346 but was continually being captured by the Lords of the Isles. For a time held by the Grants, the castle was abandoned in 1692.

# Orkney
# and Shetland

# ⌂ *Muness Castle*

| | |
|---|---|
| *Location* | Muness, Island of Unst, Shetland. |
| | OS Map 1: HP 629011. |
| *Facilities* | None. |
| *Owner* | Historic Scotland. |
| *Tel* | 0131 668 8800. |
| *Open* | All Year, Mon-Sun. |
| *Entry* | Free. |

Muness is Scotland's most northerly castle. It stands on a low ridge on the east side of the island of Unst and was built for Laurence Bruce, uncle of the Earl of Orkney. He had been implicated in a murder which took place in his native Perthshire, so he headed north to escape justice. He built this castle from 1596 until his death, with his son Andrew completing it. It remained occupied for around a century before being abandoned, and it is said to have been burned by French pirates.

The castle is rectangular in plan, the central block rather elongated at 74ft by 28ft, with round towers adjoining at diagonally opposite corners. Corbelled turrets are located at the other second floor angles. The entrance doorway is adorned with a rhyming verse and carved arms. The walls have many shot-holes in them. The entrance passage and ground floor rooms are all vaulted. The kitchen is located at the west end, having a large fireplace with bread oven, stone sink with slop drain, and a store in the round tower. Three other vaults are located in the main block, with a circular store in the south-east tower. One of these vaults was probably the wine cellar, for it has a lesser stair to the great hall. A wide scale and platt stair leads to the first floor, and the location of the great hall. Off it at either end are two private rooms, with lesser rooms in the towers. The main stair, as well as a lesser spiral, lead to the missing second floor.

## Noltland Castle

| | |
|---|---|
| *Location* | Island of Westray, Orkney. |
| | OS Map 5: HY 429488. |
| *Facilities* | None. |
| *Owner* | Historic Scotland. |
| *Tel* | 0131 668 8800. |
| *Open* | All Year, Mon-Sun. |
| *Entry* | Free. |

This castle was erected between 1560 and 1573 by Sir Gilbert Balfour, but was never completed. Balfour was involved in many scandals of the period, including the murders of Lord Darnley and Cardinal Beaton, and probably came north for safety. The castle was built on the Z-plan, with over seventy gunloops for defence, another indication of how threatened he felt. It is distinguished by its string course, which goes round the windows, and the corbel courses on the tall tower. The walls are up to seven feet thick, with dressings of sandstone which are thought to have been brought from Eday. The castle was occupied in 1650 by some soldiers from Montrose's army but was taken by local Covenanters. It was burned thereafter and abandoned.

Internally the castle boasts a fine spiral staircase in the south-west tower, with the finial at the top of the newel finely carved. At the foot of the stair is a guardroom, with a gunloop through the newel to watch the door. A passage leads to the vaulted ground-floor kitchen, which has a large fireplace and oven, and a small stair to the service area for the great hall. Either stair brings one to the main room in the castle, 62ft by 24ft, which has a fine moulded fireplace and stone window seats. A private room is located off this, with lesser spiral stairs to the second floor. Remains of the courtyard wall and gate are fragmentary.

## Scalloway Castle

| | |
|---|---|
| *Location* | Scalloway, Shetland. |
| | OS Map 4: HU 404392, |
| *Facilities* | None. |
| *Owner* | Historic Scotland. |
| *Tel* | 0131 668 8800. |
| *Open* | All year, Mon-Sun. |
| *Entry* | Free. |

Standing by the harbour of the small town of Scalloway, this tower house dates from 1600. It was erected by Patrick Stewart, Earl of Orkney. It was garrisoned by Cromwell's soldiers during the Commonwealth years. L-shaped in plan, the castle is virtually entire to the wallheads, and is four storeys in total. The castle is attractive externally. The corner turrets have fine corbels, and the north-east angle has an unusual corbelled stair. The dressed stone is Eday sandstone.

The doorway is located in the inner re-entrant, over which are a number of worn panels. To the right is the vaulted kitchen passage, which gives access to the kitchen and store, both of which are vaulted. The kitchen has a large fireplace on one side, and the well is located within the heart of the castle at the other. In the corner tower is a wide scale and platt stairway, under vaults, with a guardroom to one side. The stair rises to the great hall on the first floor, and measures 45ft by 22ft. A fine fireplace is located in the long wall, with aumbries in the ingoes. In the stair tower is a small room thought to have been the porter's lodge. Small spiral stairs at opposite ends lead to the second floor, which was occupied by bedrooms, and a second turnpike to the third floor, also bedrooms.

There is an exhibition of the history of the castle within the vaults.

# Perth
and Kinross

# Balhousie Castle

| | |
|---|---|
| *Location* | Hay Street, Perth. |
| | OS Maps 53, 58: NO 114244. |
| *Facilities* | ▯ ▲ ⚓ ♿ 🅿 |
| *Owner* | Black Watch (Royal Highland Regiment). |
| *Tel* | 01738 621281 ext. 8530. |
| *Open* | Easter-Sep, Mon-Sat; Oct-Easter, Mon-Fri. |
| *Entry* | Free. |

The Balhousie Castle which one sees today is basically a neo-baronial mansion of 1862, designed by David Smart and built for the Earl of Kinnoull. The entrance is located in the re-entrant tower, over which are Hay armorial panels. A turnpike on the east side of the castle leads to the first floor, from where a straight stair leads to the second floor. The castle is typical of the baronial style, with pepper-pot turrets at the corners, tripartite windows, elaborate bays, corbie-stepped gables and various string-courses.

If one walks to the east facade, which overlooks the North Inch, one can make out the original castle, the stonework not being so fine. Here one can see the turnpike stair, the thickness causing a projection in the wall, corbelled out at first floor level. The ancient castle of Balhousie was owned by the Eviots, but in 1625 was acquired by Francis Hay.

The castle was acquired by the army after World War II and since 1962 has been the headquarters and regimental museum of the Black Watch. There are seven museum rooms open to the public, crammed with all sorts of memorabilia, medals, pictures and uniforms.

# ⌂ *Balvaird Castle*

| | |
|---|---|
| *Location* | Balvaird, Abernethy, Perthshire. |
| | OS Map 58: NO 170115. |
| *Facilities* | ♿ |
| *Owner* | Historic Scotland. |
| *Tel* | 0131 668 8800. |
| *Open* | All Year. |
| *Entry* | Free. |

Balvaird is a most attractive tower house perched on a low knoll of the eastern Ochil Hills. It is reached by a track from the public road. Built with sandstone dressings, the tower is complete but only open occasionally. The courtyard buildings are accessible, but are in ruins. The tower is of the L-plan, with entrance door in the re-entrant. The wall-head has a corbelled parapet, and the turret corbels have small faces below them. Another carved face is located on the north wall. Within the hall is an aumbry which was probably taken from a monastery. There is a pit in the vaulted ground floor, and the latrines are all connected to one chute, flushed with water which is diverted from the roof. A cap-house at the top of the stairway gives access to the parapet walk. To the east of the castle is the former pleasance, or orchard, and the garden lies to the south.

The castle was built in 1500 by Sir Andrew Murray, who married the Barclay heiress. The courtyard range and vaulted gateway were added in 1567, with guard room. The Murrays became Viscounts Stormont and Earls of Mansfield, moving to Scone Palace, but this castle remains in their ownership, though it is in state care.

# 🏰 *Blair Castle*

| | |
|---|---|
| *Location* | Blair Atholl, Pitlochry, Perthshire, PH18 5TL. |
| | OS Map 43: NN 856662. |
| *Facilities* | 🏠🛈🍴🚻♿🅿✕🎁 |
| *Owner* | Blair Castle Trust. |
| *Tel* | 01796 481207. |
| *Open* | Apr-Oct, Mon-Sun. |
| *Entry* | ◑ |

This vast baronial mansion has 32 rooms open to the public, ranging from tiny turrets to the large dining room and ballroom. Every one is packed with the Murray family's collection of treasures and lesser artefacts built up over many centuries. These include things as diverse as Jacobite relics to a Norwegian sleigh. There is a wide selection of paintings, tapestries, arms, lace embroidery and china. The first castle was built in 1269 by the Cumming family and part of this still survives. In 1457 Blair was granted to Sir John Stewart of Balvenie by James II. It passed to the Murrays in 1629. The castle was extended in 1503, but in 1768 it was partially demolished and rebuilt as a Georgian mansion, known as Atholl House. However, in 1869 David Bryce remodelled the castle in its current neo-baronial manner and copied the entrance tower from Fyvie Castle. The white-painted towers and turrets are visible for miles around.

The castle was attacked by Cromwell's men in 1633. In 1746 Blair was attacked by General Lord George Murray to remove the Hanoverians, the last British castle to suffer a siege. The Duke of Atholl is the only person in Britain to retain a private army, the Atholl Highlanders, who parade on certain days throughout the year.

# ⌂ *Burleigh Castle*

| | |
|---|---|
| *Location* | Milnathort, Kinross-shire. |
| | OS Map 58: NO 129046. |
| *Facilities* | None. |
| *Owner* | Historic Scotland. |
| *Tel* | 0131 668 8800. |
| *Open* | All Year, Mon-Sun. |
| *Entry* | Free. |

Burleigh Castle stands by the roadside, east of Milnathort. Built of red sandstone, the original tower of c. 1500 still stands today together with a small tower dated 1582 and a stretch of connecting curtain wall, with a gateway through it. The remainder of the barmkin has long since been removed, as have lesser buildings which were built against the wall.

The old tower has a vaulted basement and a stairway to the first floor located in the north-east corner which projects into the rooms. The upper floors are gone, but large corbels for carrying the joists survive, some with masons' marks. There are garderobes off the two upper floors.

The second tower is basically circular in plan, but a small stairway projects outwith the circumference. On the second floor the tower is corbelled out to the square, to support the surviving roof. The arms of Sir James Balfour of Pittendreich and Margaret Balfour of Burleigh adorn a skewputt. The Balfours owned Burleigh from 1446. King James IV was a regular visitor at one time. In 1709 the Master of Burleigh was sentenced to death for murdering the dominie of Inverkeithing, but he escaped from prison dressed as his sister. He later became a fervent Jacobite and, in disgrace, his Baron of Burleigh title was attaint until 1868.

## Castle Menzies

| | |
|---|---|
| *Location* | Weem, Aberfeldy, Perthshire, PH15 2SD. OS Map 52: NN 837496. |
| *Facilities* | 🏠⛰🏛🐾🍴 |
| *Owner* | Menzies Charitable Trust (Menzies Clan Society). |
| *Tel* | 01887 820982. |
| *Open* | Apr-Oct, Mon-Sun. |
| *Entry* | ⬤ |

Castle Menzies is a particularly fine Z-plan tower house of c.1571-7, built of local stone with blue slate dressings. It replaced a castle burned to the ground in 1502. The decorative Victorian porch leads to the ground floor of the main block, which is a series of vaulted chambers. These include a kitchen (with a huge hearth containing a bread oven), a slop chute, stores, pantry and guard rooms. A selection of relics associated with the kitchens are on display. The wide spiral stair leads from the original entrance, complete with yett, to the first floor. Here is the great hall, with 18th-century decoration and portraits of notable Menzies. The ceiling commemorates the Union of 1707. The adjoining withdrawing room has a 17th-century plaster ceiling and Victorian pine panelling. Prince Charlie's Room is where the Young Pretender slept two nights en route to Culloden, on 4th and 5th February 1746. The main room has a restored plaster ceiling and a selection of museum cases. The anteroom contains a display of objects which includes Bonnie Prince Charlie's death mask, Bibles, bells, and pewter ware. The tower bedchamber has a wall-chamber with strong room below. The third floor has a large gallery in the roof-space, with access to the four round turrets which are a distinctive feature of the exterior. A passage leads to the west wing of 1840, designed by William Burn, which is being restored. On the ground floor is a tearoom in what was once the servants' parlour.

Externally the building is noted for its decorative pediments, armorial panels and numerous shot holes.

Castle Menzies was built on ancient Menzies homelands and was owned by the chiefs until 1918. After passing through various hands it was acquired by the Menzies Clan Society in 1957, from which time restoration work has taken place.

## Elcho Castle

| Location | Easter Elcho, Rhynd, Perthshire. |
|---|---|
| | OS Maps 53, 58: NO 165211. |
| Facilities | |
| Owner | Historic Scotland. |
| Tel | 0131 668 8800. |
| Open | Apr-Sep, Mon-Sun. |
| Entry | |

A most attractive and elaborate tower, Elcho stands on a low rock overlooking the Tay. Built in the latter half of the 16th century for the Wemyss family, it is still owned by the Earl of Wemyss and March, though it has been in state care since 1929. There are remains of a courtyard, with a chapel and a round tower with a kiln. West of the castle is an old orchard. An old quarry on the north front of the castle may have been the source for the stone, but where the dressed stone came from is unknown. An old doocot is positioned near the farm. The doorway, with yett, in the re-entrant leads to the ground floor which has three vaults – the kitchen with a serving hatch and a bread oven and cellars. A wide turnpike leads to the first floor, where the great hall and the laird's chamber are. Three lesser turnpikes lead to the upper floors, a number of which are missing, though old joists survive. The stairs reach the parapet walks, with two small rooms with fireplaces at the tower heads which are reached from the wall-walk.

The castle has a wide selection of latrines, one of which is located at the top of a turnpike stair, and another is in the north wallhead like a small outside privy!

## Huntingtower Castle

| | |
|---|---|
| *Location* | Huntingtower, by Perth. |
| | OS Maps 52, 53, 58: NO 083251. |
| *Facilities* | |
| *Owner* | Historic Scotland. |
| *Tel* | 01738 627231. |
| *Open* | Apr-Oct, Mon-Sun; Oct-Mar, Sat-Thu. |
| *Entry* | |

Originally known as Ruthven Castle, there were actually two towers here, standing side by side. In the 17th century these were joined when the space was built up, but from the inside the two distinct towers can be seen. The entrance is made to the east tower, by a vaulted room on the ground floor. The first floor hall has unique painted ceilings and walls dating from the 16th entury. The turnpike continues to the battlement walk, where the roof is slated with slabs of stone. A wooden ramp connects with the first floor of the west tower, the ground floor being the custodian's flat. The wooden floors are missing here, but the turnpike can be climbed to the parapet, which has a small doocot and cap-house. This tower is home to 200 bats.

Ruthven Castle was built in the 15th century by the Ruthvens, and the western tower was erected in the early-16th century, perhaps for their heir. In 1600 the castle was confiscated by the Crown following the Gowrie Conspiracy. It was renamed Huntingtower, and the Murrays were installed as keepers. They acquired the castle in 1663, becoming Dukes of Atholl, and used the building in preference to Blair Castle. Sold in 1805, the castle was taken into state care in 1912.

## Lochleven Castle

| Location | Castle Island, Loch Leven, Kinross-shire. |
| --- | --- |
| | OS Map 58: NO 137018. |
| Facilities | |
| Owner | Historic Scotland. |
| Tel | 01786 450000. |
| Open | Apr-Sep, Mon-Sun. |
| Entry | |

A nine-minute ferry trip from Kinross brings one to Castle Island. The castle comprises a 14th-century square keep with curtain walling. The gateway in the wall leads to the courtyard, and a doorway leads into the vaulted ground floor of the tower. A modern stair leads up to the first floor, site of a kitchen, with slop drain and garderobe. The original entrance was on the second floor. The third floor, now gone, was used as Mary, Queen of Scots' prison cell from

17 June 1567 until 2 May 1568. She had visited previously, in 1563, and on her honeymoon in 1565. One window has an oratory.

The curtain wall has steps up to a viewpoint, and at the south-east corner is the circular Glassin Tower, built around 1550. This has four storeys. A kitchen on the ground floor has a water intake and slop chute. Gunloops overlook the exterior walls. The foundations of a hall, kitchen and other buildings can be seen within the courtyard, and a dough trough is located in a large fireplace. Outwith the main gate is a bakehouse and two small cannon.

Lochleven Castle was built by the Douglases, who held it until 1672. It was later owned by the Bruces, Grahams and Montgomerys. It was taken into state care in 1939.

# Stirling
# and Central

# ⌂ *Alloa Tower*

| | |
|---|---|
| *Location* | Earn Court, Alloa Park, Alloa, Clackmannanshire, FK10 1PP. |
| | OS Map 58: NS 889925. |
| *Facilities* | 🏠 ⚑ ✿ |
| *Owner* | National Trust for Scotland. |
| *Tel* | 01259 211701. |
| *Open* | Easter; May-Sep, Mon-Sun. |
| *Entry* | ◔ |

One of the largest towers in Scotland, Alloa Tower has had a chequered history. Built in the 14th century, it was added to at various periods. A mansion was attached in the 18th century, but when it burned down in August 1800, its replacement was located elsewhere. The Georgian entrance leads to the ground floor, which has a model of a proposed new house, and a circular trap door to the dungeon. A wide turnpike stair leads to the first floor, with its minstrels' gallery and access to the 22 ft-deep well. A small turnpike leads up to the groin vaulted Charter Room, and the solar on the 3rd floor. Here is a spectacular mediaeval oak roof, window seating and aumbries. The stair continues up to the cap-house and parapet walk, which gives fine views. There are five open bartizans and a small open latrine.

The tower has a fine selection of portraits and landscapes by David Allan, Sir Henry Raeburn, and others, and a few items of furniture.

The lands of Alloa were granted to the Erskines in 1363, but the tower remained the property of the family until 1988. Mary, Queen of Scots visited in 1565 and granted the family the Earldom of Mar.

Tradition states that her infant son, Prince James (later James VI) actually died here in 1566 and was substituted with an Erskine child. The tower was restored between 1988-96 and transferred to the National Trust.

## Castle Campbell

| | |
|---|---|
| *Location* | Dollar, Clackmannanshire, FK14 7PP. |
| | OS Map 58: NS 961993. |
| *Facilities* | ▢ ♠ & ♨ ☕ |
| *Owner* | National Trust for Scotland/Historic Scotland. |
| *Tel* | 01259 472408. |
| *Open* | Apr-Sep, Mon-Sun; Oct-Mar, Sat-Thu. |
| *Entry* | ◔ |

A winding road up Dollar Glen leads to the entrance gateway of Castle Campbell, spectacularly sited on a promontory of rock. The 15th-century tower stands to the left, with a vaulted room on the ground floor, a vaulted great hall over this with a large fireplace, and a prison with pit below. The second floor has a wooden ceiling and a garderobe in the wall. The third floor is also vaulted, with decorative ribs and two grotesque masks on the ceiling. All these floors are reached by a later turnpike stairway in a tower, which also leads onto the battlements and a view down to Dollar.

The south range, which has five vaulted cellars, is mostly ruinous, but had a great hall on the first floor. Connecting this hall with the tower is the east range, c.1600, vaulted on the ground floor. It is still inhabited on the upper floors. It has a dressed masonry loggia and galleries, which are most unusual features. A vaulted passage leads through the south range to the gardens and John Knox's pulpit. Knox, the great reformer, is reputed to have preached here in the 16th century.

Castle Campbell was originally known as Castle Gloom, but in 1490 the 1st Earl of Argyll had the name changed. It was burned in 1654 by General Monk and abandoned. It was presented to the National Trust in 1950 by J.E. Kerr of Harviestoun.

# Doune Castle

| | |
|---|---|
| *Location* | Doune, Perthshire. |
| | OS Map 57: NN 728010. |
| *Facilities* | 📷 ♿ 🚻 |
| *Owner* | Earl of Moray/Historic Scotland. |
| *Tel* | 01786 841742. |
| *Open* | Apr-Sep, Mon-Sun; Oct-Mar, Sat-Thu. |
| *Entry* | ☛ |

The great castle of Doune stands on a promontory between the River Teith and Ardoch Burn. The castle was built for the Duke of Albany sometime in the 14th century and comprises two main towers with a great hall connecting them. On the south side is a large courtyard with tall walls, originally planned to have contained domestic buildings, the windows of which were formed. The well is within the courtyard. The west tower contains the kitchen with a huge fireplace and impressive servery. The great hall has a high wooden ceiling with corbels carved into faces, a minstrel's gallery, brazier and old furniture. Externally, the water from the roof is shed by ornate gargoyles. The inner hall was restored in 1883 by George Stuart, 14th Earl of

Moray. It has a double fireplace, minstrels' gallery and some furniture made from the gallows tree of Doune, which was blown over in 1878. The upper hall above contains a small chapel.

Doune passed from the Albany family to the Crown in 1424. In 1525 it was given by Margaret Tudor to Henry Stewart, Lord Methven, before passing by marriage to the Stuarts. It is still owned by the Earls of Moray, but was leased to Historic Scotland for 999 years.

## Menstrie Castle

| | |
|---|---|
| *Location* | Castle Road, Menstrie, Clackmannanshire, FK10. OS Map 58: NS 851968. |
| *Facilities* | None. |
| *Owner* | Clackmannanshire Council/NTS. |
| *Tel* | 01259 213131. |
| *Open* | Easter; May-Sep, Sat-Sun. |
| *Entry* | Free. |

Now located in the midst of a housing scheme, most of this castle has been subdivided into flats. Externally the structure comprises random rubble, with corner turrets, and a vaulted pend through the middle of the building. The ground floor to the left of the gateway is now the Nova Scotia Commemoration Room and it is this which is open to the public. Connected to it is a vaulted room. The connection with Nova Scotia, the Canadian state, is due to the fact that Sir William Alexander, 1st Earl of Stirling, was born here in 1567. He was James VI's Lieutenant for the plantation of Nova Scotia and a noted poet. The room is adorned with displays on the history of this scheme, as well as painted armorials depicting the 109 Nova Scotian baronetcies created as a result. These were sold for three thousand Scots merks (£166.66) each. There are also portraits of James VI, Charles I and Sir William.

Menstrie was bought in 1649 by Sir James Holbourne and sold in 1719 to Alexander Abercromby. Sir Ralph Abercromby (1734-1801), who commanded the British Army at Aboukir Bay, was born here.

The castle was saved from demolition in 1957 when a fund was launched to restore it. The architect was Schomberg Scott and it was opened to the public in 1961.

## Stirling Castle

| | |
|---|---|
| *Location* | Castlehill, Stirling, FK8 1EJ. |
| | OS Map 57: NS 790941. |
| *Facilities* | ▢ ▲ ⚑ ⚕ ♨ ✕ ⚑ |
| *Owner* | Historic Scotland. |
| *Tel* | 01786 450000. |
| *Open* | All Year, Mon-Sun. |
| *Entry* | ⬤ |

Stirling is a large and impressive castle built on the rock above the town. There are many buildings to explore, and the castle's history extends from earliest times to the present. A bridge over the outer ditch leads to the outer defences, followed by the forework. To the left is the Lion's Den and gardens, with the Queen Anne Battery of 1708. The next gateway leads through to the lower square with the palace block to the left, which has fine external statuary. The great hall stands in front and to the right are the foundations and vaults of the Elphinstone Tower. Between the palace and great hall a passage leads to the upper square, with the King's Old Building to the left (now the Argyll and Sutherland Highlanders' Regimental Headquarters and Museum), and the former Chapel Royal. A wall-walk can be followed round much of the castle, and at one point it bears the initials of various royals. From it can be seen the King's Knot, an ornamental garden, which may date from 1628.

The history of Stirling Castle is tied to the history of Scotland. It has been in Royal hands since construction, though after 1746 was used as a barracks until 1964. There is much restoration work underway.

# The Western Isles

#  *Kisimul Castle*

| | |
|---|---|
| *Location* | Castlebay, Island of Barra, HS9. |
| | OS Map 31: NL 665979. |
| *Facilities* | None. |
| *Owner* | MacNeil of Barra. |
| *Tel* | 01871 810336. |
| *Open* | May-Sep, Wed, Sat. |
| *Entry* | ◖ |

Sometimes spelled Kiessimul, or Kismull, this castle is famous as the seat of the MacNeils of Barra. It stands on an islet in Castle Bay and a small boat plies visitors to and fro. The original castle is said to date from 1120, though some accounts date construction to post-1427. The castle has undergone many restorations and alterations, however. It was abandoned in the mid-18th century and burned in 1795. For a long time a ruin, the 45th chief, Robert Lister MacNeil, an American architect, restored the building between 1938 and 1970.

The castle occupies the whole of the island, with the walls taking the shape of the shoreline. The main gateway is reached by steps from the shore, with a modern coat of arms and machicolation over. A wall encloses a small courtyard, within which is the old castle well. Lower buildings – the chapel, north tower, great hall and the 1950s Tanist House – are located against the curtain wall, the north corner having a turret. The great tower dates from the 14th century and rises five storeys in height. The base of the external walls are splayed. The ground floor contains a store. A wooden stair and platform give access to the first floor. Ladders within allow one to go up and down. On view are a garderobe and aumbries. The castle has many Clan MacNeil mementoes.

# Castles Open Irregularly
# Or By Appointment

The following castles, generally in private ownership and occupied in most cases, are open to the public either at irregular times, or else by appointment. Usually, in the case of those which are open by prior arrangement, at least two-to-three days notice is required, if not longer, so if holidaying in an area, it is best to arrange a visit before travelling.

## *Balfluig Castle*

| | |
|---|---|
| *Location* | Alford, Aberdeenshire, AB33 8EJ. |
| | OS Map 37: NJ 586150. |
| *Owner* | Mark I. Tennant. |
| *Tel* | 0171 624 3200. |
| *Open* | By written appointment. |

Dating from 1556, Balfluig is an L-plan tower house, built by the Forbes family. It was sold to the Farquharsons in 1753 and became a farmhouse which was then abandoned until restoration work took place in 1966-7. The ground floor is vaulted, and a turnpike stair in an external re-entrant leads up to the great hall on the first floor.

## *Castle Stalcaire*

| | |
|---|---|
| *Location* | Portnacroish, Appin, Oban, Argyll. |
| | OS Map 49: NM 920473. |
| *Owner* | Mrs M. Stewart Allward. |
| *Tel* | 01883 622768/01631 730234. |
| *Open* | By arrangement. |
| *Entry* | ◗ |

Located on a tiny islet in coastal Loch Laich, Castle Stalcaire (or Stalker) had restoration work begun in 1965. The tower dates from the 15th century, with some walls being nine feet thick, though the upper works are dated 1631. There was a small courtyard on the south side. The castle was built by Duncan Stewart and remained in his family until 1765.

## *Claypotts Castle*

| | |
|---|---|
| *Location* | Broughty Ferry, Dundee, Angus. |
| | OS Map 54: NO 453319. |
| *Owner* | Historic Scotland. |
| *Tel* | 01786 450000. |
| *Open* | Limited opening. |
| *Entry* | ☺ |

Claypotts is a delight. The rectangular central block is flanked on opposite corners by two round towers which are corbelled out to the square at roof level. Two turnpikes are located in the angles and the open battlements are unusual features. The castle dates from 1569-88, being built by the Strachans, though ownership passed to John Graham of Claverhouse.

## *Comlongon Castle*

| | |
|---|---|
| *Location* | Clarencefield, Dumfries, DG1 4NA. |
| | OS Map 85: NY 079689 |
| *Owner* | Phillip and Simon Ptolemy. |
| *Tel* | 01387 870283. |
| *Open* | By appointment. |

The massive tower, rising 75ft in height, was erected in 1450 by Sir Cuthbert Murray of Cockpool. The Murray family owned Comlongon for centuries, being Wardens of the West March, and latterly became Earls of Mansfield. The castle was sold by the 8th Earl in 1984 to Tony Ptolemy. An adjoining mansion is now a hotel. The castle used to be open regularly, but is closed currently due to safety problems.


## *Coxton Tower*

| | |
|---|---|
| *Location* | Coxton, Lhanbryde, Elgin, Moray, IV30 3QS. |
| | OS Map 29: NJ262607. |
| *Owner* | Roger and Malcolm Christie. |
| *Tel* | 01343 842225. |
| *Open* | By appointment; donations welcomed. |

Coxton was one of the last tower houses to be built in Scotland, and was finished in 1644 by Sir Alexander Innes. It is a small square tower, rising to four storeys, with turrets and open battlements at opposite corners. The rooms are vaulted, and the roof is constructed of stone slabs, because of Innes's fear of fire. The entrance was originally on the first floor, to which stairs were added in the 19th century.

## Craigston Castle

| | |
|---|---|
| *Location* | Turriff, Aberdeenshire, OS Map 29: NJ 762550. |
| *Owner* | William P. Urquhart. |
| *Tel* | 01888 551228. |
| *Open* | A few weeks in summer or by arrangement. |

Built by John Urquhart in 1604-7, the massive white tower of Craigston is a striking edifice with its sandstone fenestrations and ornate balcony. At the top is a balustraded viewing tower. Within the drawing room are fine wooden carvings depicting Biblical themes. Also on show are the great hall and several bedrooms. Apart from an 80 year period, the castle has always been owned by the Urquharts.

## Ferniehirst Castle

| | |
|---|---|
| *Location* | Jedburgh, Roxburghshire. OS Map 80: NT 652180. |
| *Owner* | Marquess of Lothian. |
| *Tel* | 01835 862201. |
| *Open* | By appointment. |

A fine L-plan tower house, Ferniehirst was restored between 1984-7 after 50 years' use as a Youth Hostel. It has a modern thatched extension. On show are the panelled entrance hall, the Hall of History which has modern friezes, the grand apartment and the turret library. Open on Wednesday afternoons during the summer are the Kerr museum (located in the 16th-century chapel) and two vaults of the castle, one of which is a modern chapel.

## Gilnockie Tower

| | |
|---|---|
| *Location* | Canonbie, Dumfriesshire, DG14 0XD. |
| | OS Map 85: NY 382785. |
| *Owner* | Colin Armstrong. |
| *Tel* | 01387 371876. |
| *Open* | Tours all year at 10.00 and 14.30. |

Gilnockie, sometimes called Hollows, stands in the valley of the River Esk, two miles north of Canonbie. For many years a ruin, it was re-roofed in 1979-80 and again lived in. The tower rises four storeys in height, plus attic, and was the home of Johnnie Armstrong, the hero of many Border ballads, who was hanged by James V in 1530. The ground floor is vaulted, and a turnpike stair is located in the south-west corner.

## Kilravock Castle

| | |
|---|---|
| *Location* | Croy, Inverness, IV1 2PJ. |
| | OS Map 27: NH 814493. |
| *Owner* | Miss Elizabeth Rose. |
| *Tel* | 01667 493258. |
| *Open* | May-Sep, Wed. Groups by appointment. |

A great stone keep erected in 1460, Kilravock has been the seat of the

Rose (sometimes spelled Ross in history) family ever since. It was extended in the 17th century. Notable visitors include Mary, Queen of Scots, Bonnie Prince Charlie and Robert Burns. Guided tours are given of the castle, and afternoon teas are on sale.

## Minard Castle

| | |
|---|---|
| *Location* | Minard, by Inveraray, Argyll, PA32 8YB. |
| | OS Map 55: NR 972942. |
| *Owner* | Reinold Gayre. |
| *Tel* | 01546 886272. |
| *Open* | By appointment. |
| *Entry* | ◑ |

Located on a headland in Loch Fyne, the oldest part of the house was built by the Campbells in the 18th century. This was extended in the 19th century in a Tudoresque style by the addition of a new castellated front.

The castle was owned for a time by Thomas Lloyd (1835-1905), whose memorial stands in the village. For a number of years the castle operated as a hotel, but was purchased by the Gayre family as a private home in 1974.

## Monzie Castle

| | |
|---|---|
| *Location* | Crieff, Perthshire, PH7 4HD. |
| | OS Maps 52/58: NN 873245. |
| *Owner* | Mrs C.M.M. Crichton. |
| *Tel* | 01764 653110. |
| *Open* | May-Jun, Mon-Sun; other times by appointment. |
| *Entry* | ◐ |

Monzie comprises two distinct buildings adjoining each other. The older part is an L-planned tower of 1634, rising to two storeys. Bulkier and finely furnished is the 1791-5 castle which was designed by John Paterson. The castle was partially burned in 1908 but was restored by Sir Robert Lorimer.

## *Sorn Castle*

| | |
|---|---|
| *Location* | Sorn, Mauchline, Ayrshire, KA5 6HR. |
| | OS Map 70: NS 548269. |
| *Owner* | Mrs Anne MacIntyre. |
| *Tel* | 01292 268181. |
| *Open* | By appointment. |
| *Entry* | ⬤ |

The old tower dates from the 15th century and has been extended on a number of occasions. Guests are shown a number of rooms, including the dining room, billiard room, and library. On show are some relics of the Covenanters. Sorn was built by the Hamiltons, but the castle passed to the Campbells of Loudoun in 1680 and since 1903 has been in MacIntyre hands, whose arms are displayed on an external wall.

## Towie Barclay Castle

| | |
|---|---|
| *Location* | Fyvie, Aberdeenshire. |
| | OS Map 29: NJ745439. |
| *Owner* | Marc Ellington. |
| *Tel* | 01888 511347. |
| *Open* | By appointment. |

The L-planned tower was built in the 16th century by the Barclay family. Ruinous for many years, it was restored in the 1970s. The tower is harled and has sandstone quoins, and there is a small formal garden. The doorway leads to the small hall, off which are vaults containing a kitchen, dining room and bedroom. On the first floor is a fine Gothic vaulted great hall with a richly furnished minstrels' gallery.

# Castles In Care

These castles are currently closed and entry is not possible. However, it is possible to view the exterior elevations.

# Auchindoun Castle

| | |
|---|---|
| *Location* | Auchindoun, Dufftown, Banffshire. |
| | OS Map 29: NJ 349374. |
| *Owner* | Historic Scotland. |
| *Tel* | 0131 668 8800. |

Auchindoun is an extensive ruin comprising a 15th-century tower, courtyard and outbuildings. The castle was built by the Earl of Mar but passed into Ogilvie and Gordon hands, witnessing sieges and sackings a number of times. It was abandoned by the early-18th century.

# Cadzow Castle

| | |
|---|---|
| *Location* | Chatelherault, Ferniegair, Hamilton, Lanarkshire. |
| | OS Map 64: NS 734537, |
| *Owner* | South Lanarkshire Council/Historic Scotland. |
| *Tel* | 0131 668 8800/01698 426213. |

Perched high above the gorge of the Avon Water, Cadzow is located in the attractive Chatelherault country park. The castle was left for a long time as a romantic ruin within the Duke of Hamilton's policies, but consolidation work is underway to make it safe for visitors. The castle was erected of red sandstone betwen 1500-50 by Sir James Hamilton of Finnart for his half-brother, the 2nd Earl of Arran.

# Castle Girnigoe and Sinclair

| | |
|---|---|
| *Location* | Noss, Wick, Caithness. |
| | OS Map 12: ND 379549. |
| *Owner* | Wick Society/Castle Girnigoe & Sinclair Task Force. |
| *Tel* | 01955 605393. |

The ruins are dangerous, but are worth looking at from nearby, as they are perched on a wild headland. Castle Girnigoe is the older structure, dating from the 15th century. Castle Sinclair was built in Girnigoe's courtyard between 1606-7, but both were damaged in a siege of 1679 and abandoned. Both were Sinclair properties.

# Castle of Park

| Location | Glenluce, Wigtownshire. |
| --- | --- |
| | OS Map 82: NX 188571. |
| Owner | Historic Scotland. |
| Tel | 0131 668 8800. |

This simple tower house was erected between 1590-99 by Thomas Hay. Rising four storeys in height, the castle is L-shaped in plan. The ground floor is vaulted; the main stair located in the jamb. Lesser turnpikes are located in the upper floors. The castle was restored internally between 1992-3.

## *Clackmannan Tower*

*Location*   Clackmannan, Clackmannanshire.
            OS Map 58: NS 907919.
*Owner*      Historic Scotland.
*Tel*        0131 668 8800.

Located on a hill, Clackmannan commands a wide view. The tower was erected in the 14th century and extended in the 15th century. The ground and first floors are vaulted. The tower was a Bruce property until 1796. Part of the tower collapsed because of mining subsidence, but has since been rebuilt.

## *Inverlochy Castle*

*Location*   Inverlochy, Fort William, Inverness-shire.
            OS Map 41: NN 120754.
*Owner*      Historic Scotland.
*Tel*        0131 668 8800.

Built by the Comyns, Inverlochy is one of Scotland's oldest stone castles, dating from the 13th century. It passed to the Gordons. It comprises a square courtyard with round towers at the corners, the largest of which was the keep. The castle is subject to long-term consolidation work.

## Preston Tower

| | |
|---|---|
| *Location* | Prestonpans, East Lothian. |
| | OS Map 66: NT 390741. |
| *Owner* | National Trust for Scotland/East Lothian Council. |
| *Tel* | 0131 226 5922. |

Now surrounded by housing, Preston Tower dates from the 15th century. It was burned out by Cromwell's forces in 1650 after which it was restored and extended upward with a fine Renaissance attic tower. The castle has a small garden, in which is a 17th-century doocot. Originally built by the Hamiltons, the castle was acquired by the Trust in 1969.

## Rowallan Castle

| | |
|---|---|
| *Location* | Rowallan, Kilmaurs, Kilmarnock, Ayrshire. |
| | OS Map 70: NS 435424. |
| *Owner* | Historic Scotland. |
| *Tel* | 0131 668 8800. |

Rowallan is a fine courtyard building, most of which is still roofed. Twin towers guard the entrance passage which has a guardroom off it. The castle has numerous decorative features, including cable-mouldings, armorial panels, gunloops and decorative stonework. The castle was built by the Mures but was later owned by the Earls of Glasgow and Earls of Loudoun before being acquired by the Corbett Lords Rowallan.

# Glossary

| | |
|---|---|
| armorial panel | stone panel bearing a coat of arms or crest. |
| aumbry | cupboard, dresser, safe, or recess for religious vessels. |
| barmkin | outer wall of a castle. |
| baronial | turreted style of architecture, common in Scotland. |
| bartizan | an open corner turret, usually corbelled (qv). |
| brew house | brewery, place where beer was made. |
| cap-house | small room at the top of a turnpike stair, usually giving access to the parapet walk. |
| castellated | having turrets and battlements. |
| corbel | a projecting stone on a wall which supports further building, joists, etc. |
| corbie-stepped gables | Scots crow-stepped gables. |
| dais | main end of the dining room, where the high table stood; often raised. |
| doocot | Scots dovecote. |
| double towers | twin towers, two towers side by side. |
| dressings | masonry of a better finish, usually round a window or other opening. |
| entresol | half-way floor within the height of a tall chamber, mezzanine. |
| forework | defensive walling protecting the entrance to a castle. |
| garderobe | dry closet, privy. |
| girnal | Scots meal chest. |
| gunloop | opening through a wall for a gun or cannon. |
| harl/harling | traditional Scots form of roughcast, or wet dash finish for exterior walls. |
| ingle | Scots fire, fireplace. |
| joggled lintel | lintel in which the stones are notched or jig-sawed together for additional strength. |
| laigh hall | 'low' or lesser apartment in a castle, more public than the 'Great Hall'. |
| laird's lug | secret hole through an internal wall which the laird, or landed proprietor, could use to listen to or spy on his guests. |

| | |
|---|---|
| lesser turnpike | secondary stair. |
| loggia | covered but open arcade, often colonnaded on one side. |
| machicolation | opening between the corbels on a parapet through which attackers could be repelled by dropping missiles on them. |
| mangonel | mediaeval device for throwing stones. |
| murder hole | prison or pit which had no means of escape, hence all inmates dying within. |
| newel-stair | spiral stair formed round an upright column, or newel. |
| ogee moulding | moulding with S-shaped curves. |
| oratory | private room or chapel for prayer. |
| oriel | window which projects from an upper floor, often by means of corbelling. |
| pediment | triangular gable over a window or door. |
| pend | Scots vaulted passage through a building. |
| piscina | basin with drain for rinsing religious vessels. |
| porte-cochere | carriage porch, or open porch in front of a main entrance. |
| postern | back door or gate, sally-port. |
| quern | circular stone used for grinding corn. |
| quoin | corner stone on a wall, often dressed or proud of the surface. |
| re-entrant tower | tower, often containing a stair, located in the inner angle of an L-planned building. |
| shot hole | hole in wall for shooting through, cf. gun-loop. |
| skewputt | the larger stone, which is often ornamented, at the base of a row of skews, or coping stones, on a gable. |
| squinch | archway across the inner angle of perpendicular walls used to support superstructure. |
| squint | hole through a wall or pillar giving a view of a main room. |
| string-course | course of projecting moulded masonry used for decoration. |
| tracery | fine stonework subdividing a large window, often ecclesiastical. |
| tripartite window | window in three main parts, or having two mullions. |
| turnpike stair | spiral stair, cf. newel-stair. |
| wall-head | straight top of a wall. |
| yett | Scots meaning literally gate, but descriptive of a particularly Scottish form of gate comprising interlaced iron bars, located behind the main doorway of a castle. |

# Index to Main Entries

Aberdour Castle, 77
Aikwood Tower, 47
Alloa Tower, 135
Armadale Castle, 109
Auchindoun Castle, 153
Ayton Castle, 48

Balfluig Castle, 144
Balgonie Castle, 78
Balhousie Castle, 125
Ballindalloch Castle, 11
Balvaird Castle, 126
Balvenie Castle, 12
Barcaldine Castle, 35
Blackness Castle, 79
Blair Castle, 127
Bothwell Castle, 95
Braemar Castle, 13
Brodick Castle, 96
Brodie Castle, 14
Broughty Castle, 72
Burleigh Castle, 128

Cadzow Castle, 153
Caerlaverock Castle, 59
Cardoness Castle, 60
Carnasserie Castle, 36
Carsluith Castle, 61
Castle Campbell, 136
    Fraser, 15
    Girnigoe and Sinclair, 153
    Menzies, 129
    of Old Wick, 110
    of Park, 154
    of St John, 62

Stalcaire, 144
Stuart, 111
Sween, 37
Cawdor Castle, 112
Clackmannan Tower, 155
Claypotts Castle, 145
Comlongon Castle, 145
Corgarff Castle, 16
Coxton Tower, 146
Craigievar Castle, 17
Craigmillar Castle, 80
Craignethan Castle, 97
Craigston Castle, 147
Crathes Castle, 19
Crichton Castle, 81
Crookston Castle, 98
Culzean Castle, 99

Darnaway Castle, 20
Dean Castle, 100
Delgatie Castle, 21
Dirleton Castle, 82
Doune Castle, 137
Drum Castle, 22
Drumcoltran Tower, 63
Drumlanrig Castle, 64
Drumlanrig's Tower, 49
Duart Castle, 38
Duffus Castle, 23
Dumbarton Castle, 101
Dundonald Castle, 102
Dunnottar Castle, 24
Dunrobin Castle, 113
Dunstaffnage Castle, 39
Dunvegan Castle, 114

Edinburgh Castle, 83
Edzell Castle, 73
Eilean Donan Castle, 115
Elcho Castle, 130

Ferniehirst Castle, 147
Floors Castle, 50
Fyvie Castle, 25

Gilnockie Tower, 148
Glamis Castle, 74
Glenbuchat Castle, 26
Greenknowe Tower, 51

Hailes Castle, 85
Hermitage Castle, 52
Huntingtower Castle, 131
Huntly Castle, 27

Inveraray Castle, 40
Inverlochy Castle, 155

Kelburn Castle, 103
Kellie Castle, 86
Kilchurn Castle, 41
Kildrummy Castle, 28
Kilravock Castle, 148
Kisimul Castle, 142

Lauriston Castle, 87
Leith Hall, 30
Lennoxlove Castle, 88
Loch Doon Castle, 104
Lochleven Castle, 132
Lochmaben Castle, 65
Lochranza Castle, 105
MacLellan's Castle, 66
Menstrie Castle, 138

Minard Castle, 149
Monzie Castle, 149
Morton Castle, 67
Muness Castle, 120

Neidpath Castle, 53
Newark Castle, 106
Noltland Castle, 121

Orchardton Tower, 68

Preston Tower, 156
Ravenscraig Castle, 89
Rothesay Castle, 42
Rowallan Castle, 156

Scalloway Castle, 122
Scotstarvit Tower, 91
Skipness Castle, 43
Smailholm Tower, 55
Sorn Castle, 150
Spynie Castle, 31
St Andrews Castle, 90
Stirling Castle, 139
Strome Castle, 117

Tantallon Castle, 92
Thirlestane Castle, 56
Threave Castle, 69
Tolquhon Castle, 32
Torosay Castle, 44
Towie Barclay Castle, 151

Urquhart Castle, 118